S. Hrg. 113–576

PRESERVING PUBLIC SAFETY AND NETWORK RELIABILITY IN THE IP TRANSITION

HEARING

BEFORE THE

SUBCOMMITTEE ON COMMUNICATIONS, TECHNOLOGY, AND THE INTERNET

OF THE

COMMITTEE ON COMMERCE, SCIENCE, AND TRANSPORTATION UNITED STATES SENATE

ONE HUNDRED THIRTEENTH CONGRESS

SECOND SESSION

JUNE 5, 2014

Printed for the use of the Committee on Commerce, Science, and Transportation

U.S. GOVERNMENT PUBLISHING OFFICE

93–481 PDF   WASHINGTON : 2015

For sale by the Superintendent of Documents, U.S. Government Publishing Office
Internet: bookstore.gpo.gov   Phone: toll free (866) 512–1800; DC area (202) 512–1800
Fax: (202) 512–2104   Mail: Stop IDCC, Washington, DC 20402–0001

SENATE COMMITTEE ON COMMERCE, SCIENCE, AND TRANSPORTATION

ONE HUNDRED THIRTEENTH CONGRESS

SECOND SESSION

JOHN D. ROCKEFELLER IV, West Virginia, *Chairman*

BARBARA BOXER, California	JOHN THUNE, South Dakota, *Ranking*
BILL NELSON, Florida	ROGER F. WICKER, Mississippi
MARIA CANTWELL, Washington	ROY BLUNT, Missouri
MARK PRYOR, Arkansas	MARCO RUBIO, Florida
CLAIRE McCASKILL, Missouri	KELLY AYOTTE, New Hampshire
AMY KLOBUCHAR, Minnesota	DEAN HELLER, Nevada
MARK BEGICH, Alaska	DAN COATS, Indiana
RICHARD BLUMENTHAL, Connecticut	TIM SCOTT, South Carolina
BRIAN SCHATZ, Hawaii	TED CRUZ, Texas
EDWARD MARKEY, Massachusetts	DEB FISCHER, Nebraska
CORY BOOKER, New Jersey	RON JOHNSON, Wisconsin
JOHN E. WALSH, Montana	

ELLEN L. DONESKI, *Staff Director*
JOHN WILLIAMS, *General Counsel*
DAVID SCHWIETERT, *Republican Staff Director*
NICK ROSSI, *Republican Deputy Staff Director*
REBECCA SEIDEL, *Republican General Counsel and Chief Investigator*

————

SUBCOMMITTEE ON COMMUNICATIONS, TECHNOLOGY,
AND THE INTERNET

MARK PRYOR, Arkansas, *Chairman*	ROGER F. WICKER, Mississippi, *Ranking*
BARBARA BOXER, California	*Member*
BILL NELSON, Florida	ROY BLUNT, Missouri
MARIA CANTWELL, Washington	MARCO RUBIO, Florida
CLAIRE McCASKILL, Missouri	KELLY AYOTTE, New Hampshire,
AMY KLOBUCHAR, Minnesota	DEAN HELLER, Nevada
MARK BEGICH, Alaska	DAN COATS, Indiana
RICHARD BLUMENTHAL, Connecticut	TIM SCOTT, South Carolina
BRIAN SCHATZ, Hawaii	TED CRUZ, Texas
EDWARD MARKEY, Massachusetts	DEB FISCHER, Nebraska
CORY BOOKER, New Jersey	RON JOHNSON, Wisconsin
JOHN E. WALSH, Montana	

CONTENTS

WITNESSES

APPENDIX

PRESERVING PUBLIC SAFETY AND NETWORK RELIABILITY IN THE IP TRANSITION

––––––––––

THURSDAY, JUNE 5, 2014

U.S. SENATE,
SUBCOMMITTEE ON COMMUNICATIONS, TECHNOLOGY, AND
THE INTERNET,
COMMITTEE ON COMMERCE, SCIENCE, AND TRANSPORTATION,
Washington, DC.

The Subcommittee met, pursuant to notice, at 9:15 a.m. in Room SR–253, Russell Senate Office Building, Hon. Mark Pryor, Chairman of the Subcommittee, presiding.

OPENING STATEMENT OF HON. MARK PRYOR,
U.S. SENATOR FROM ARKANSAS

Senator PRYOR. Well, we will call the hearing to order. Thank you for coming to the Senate Subcommittee on Communications, Technology, and the Internet, the Committee on Commerce, Science, and Transportation.

So I want to thank all the witnesses for being here today, and we will have a number of colleagues coming and going this morning. We have a number of other hearings and markups, et cetera, going on, some action on the floor as well. So some of our colleagues will be coming and going.

So let me just say good morning to everyone, and welcome to today's hearing. We are here today to discuss the public safety and network reliability aspects of the ongoing evolution of our Nation's communications networks.

Today, the Nation's voice networks are in the midst of multiple transitions that promise to change how we communicate. First, the transmission infrastructure that carries our voice communication is moving away from reliance on copper to fiber optics. Next, the so-called "circuit-switched protocols" that have long underpinned traditional telephone service are transitioning to newer Internet protocols, or IP systems. And finally, many Americans are choosing to substitute wireless service for traditional wired voice communications.

However, there may be challenges that consumers, carriers, and the public safety officials face as our networks increasingly rely on all-IP technology and fiber optic infrastructure. For example, in my state, Arkansas recently suffered a severe tornado. Tragically, we lost 18 Arkansans in that, and significant property damage as well. Thirty-six thousand homes lost power.

I have heard nothing but very positive things from the Arkansas Department of Emergency Management and the Governor's office about how our local telephone companies reacted during and immediately after the storm. I would expect those companies in Arkansas and others around the country to continue their commitment to public safety, no matter the technology used to transmit phone calls over our networks.

Consumers have come to trust the reliability and resiliency of the old copper telephone network. They cannot afford to wait for a disaster to strike to find out that there are gaps in our communications networks in an all-IP world. So I want to be sure that we are exploring the public safety implications of these transitions and asking the right questions proactively, but also, I do want to stress that the IP transition presents an important opportunity for consumers and communication providers.

New technologies bring potential of new services and possibilities to make our networks even more efficient and to bring down costs for consumers. Rather than be an impediment to this progress, it is my intention to explore this transition in a thorough manner to identify any challenges, discuss their implications in depth, and work toward solutions in advance to mitigate any negative impacts.

So I want to recognize the efforts by the Federal Communications Commission, AT&T, and other carriers who are working with the Commission to carefully and deliberately explore the implications of the IP transition through the FCC's transition trials. Ultimately, it is my hope that through these trials, all stakeholders can work together to proactively address any issues revealed in the trials, protect consumers, and preserve public safety. But I also expect Congress to maintain close oversight over this process. A transition of this magnitude deserves nothing less.

And again, I want to thank you all again for being here, and I want to hear your perspective on this important discussion. I look forward to your testimony, and I want to turn it over to the Ranking Member, Senator Wicker.

STATEMENT OF HON. ROGER F. WICKER, U.S. SENATOR FROM MISSISSIPPI

Senator WICKER. Thank you, Chairman Pryor.

This hearing deals with preserving public safety and network reliability in the IP transition. This hearing is—it certainly hits home not only for Arkansans, but for Mississippians, who experienced devastating storms this year also.

In late April, tornados ravaged communities in Mississippi and Arkansas, taking innocent lives and causing extensive damage. Despite the devastation, we can be thankful for the technology that provided critical information ahead of time, alerting people to take shelter and saving hundreds of our fellow citizens. The swift action of our weather forecasters, local officials, and first responders validated the importance of technology and communication when disaster strikes.

The modernization of our Nation's communications network, from legacy copper line telephone infrastructure to high-speed fiber and wireless broadband, is expected to maximize the benefits of IP broadband networks to all Americans. These networks will provide far more capable and efficient voice services, allow faster and more robust data transfers, deliver 21st century education and health services, and enhance public safety communications, like Next Generation 911.

There will be a host of issues raised when we discuss IP transition, but nothing is more important than ensuring a seamless transition for our first responders and the citizens they serve and protect. The capacity for this technology to protect citizens not only must be preserved, but also improved by this exciting new transition.

The FCC has moved the ball forward in constructive ways, authorizing voluntary IP transition trials. These trials will test and analyze the impact of moving away from legacy communication networks, particularly in regard to public safety. The Commission held a public IP transition workshop in April that focused on the transition's effects on critical public safety, emergency response, and national security functions.

I would like to welcome the FCC's Chief Technology Officer, who provided important technical expertise to the workshop and is here today to do the same. I welcome the rest of our witnesses, who represent a cross-section of key stakeholders, including State and public safety officials, consumers, broadband providers themselves, who have invested significant capital and resources to deploy modern infrastructure.

I am glad we are all here today. The hearing will be brief. We are going to let you start talking.

Ensuring a smooth path for public safety must be an "all hands on deck" effort with Congress, the FCC, and stakeholders working together to scrutinize the IP transition's impact on emergency communications in this country.

So, Mr. Chairman, thank you again for holding this important hearing.

Senator PRYOR. Thank you, Senator Wicker, and I want to thank you and your staff for being flexible because, as you all know, we have moved the time here from 10 a.m., to 9:30 a.m., to 9:15 a.m., to try to accommodate Senators' schedules, and so thank you all for doing that.

We are also going to make a slight change when it comes to you all's opening statement. Mr. Schulzrinne has a presentation, which will take 5 minutes. I think we are asking everybody else to limit their remarks to 3 minutes, if we can.

So let me go ahead and introduce the whole panel. Then I will recognize Mr. Schulzrinne.

Mr. Henning Schulzrinne, Chief Technology Officer at Federal Communications Commission, will be our first witness.

Then we will have Jonathan Banks, Senior Vice President, Law and Policy, USTelecom.

Then we will have Jodie Griffin, Senior Staff Attorney, Public Knowledge.

And then we will have Colette Honorable. She is the Chair of the Board and President of the National Association of Regulatory Utility Commissioners, and she is also Chairman of the State of Arkansas's State Public Service Commission.

And Ms. Gigi Smith, President of APCO International.

So, Mr. Schulzrinne, let me recognize you for your presentation. Thank you.

STATEMENT OF HENNING SCHULZRINNE,
CHIEF TECHNOLOGY OFFICER,
FEDERAL COMMUNICATIONS COMMISSION

Mr. SCHULZRINNE. Thank you, Chairman Pryor, Ranking Member Wicker, and members of the Subcommittee.

I appreciate the opportunity to appear before you today to provide some technical context regarding the technology transitions that you referred to and, in particular, public safety. My name is Henning Schulzrinne, and I am the Chief Technology Officer for the Federal Communications Commission. As CTO, I am pleased to discuss the technical foundation for today's topic but will respectfully decline comment on any policy-related matters.

The transition to communication networks based on Internet protocols, short IP, offers an opportunity to improve emergency communications unprecedented since the conversion from analogue to digital systems in the 1970s and 1980s. However, these very same changes also pose new challenges to performance, reliability, and sustainability of emergency communication systems.

As you hinted at, about 70 percent of all 911 calls originate on a mobile phone today. And of the 79 million residential landline connections in the United States, 34 million are now interconnected Voice over IP, as opposed to TDM.

We can also no longer take for granted that all households have a TV, a landline phone with a central office battery back-up, or even a battery-powered transistor radio. Or that, say, a college student will be watching TV when the emergency alert tone sounds to seek shelter.

The transition to IP is multifaceted and encompasses three layers. At the application layer, voice, video, and text services are enabled by new Internet application layer protocols, instead of the old Signaling System No. 7. At the transport layer, IP offers an application-neutral mechanism that replaces the old-time division multiplexing foundation. The physical layer, dominated by copper loops, is integrating fiber, wireless, coax, and satellite into a unified whole.

However, even as the transition is taking place, we should not forget that large parts of the voice network are still using the same TDM technology and hardware developed and deployed, in some cases, 30 or 40 years ago, in particular for public safety, so-called CAMA trunks originally developed for operator services. Unfortunately, CAMA trunks have played a role in two large-scale outages of 911 systems in the last few years.

Spare parts, investment, and expertise needed to maintain these legacy networks are becoming scarce. Yet, as FCC Chairman Wheeler has stated, public safety is one of the core values that must be sustained during the Nation's transition to all-IP networks.

Two technical challenges that will need to be addressed in this transition are back-up power and emergency location. No longer will we have access to back-up power provided by the central office, as it has been the case for many years, but there are also new technical opportunities to leverage in-system power through user exchangeable batteries—for example, batteries that look similar to what you might have as back-up on your cell phone—or energy-efficient network termination devices that will make it possible to sustain uninterrupted communication for both voice and, increasingly important, for Internet services, even if commercial power should be disrupted.

The second topic, location technology, such as GPS, has been very successful, along with network-based triangulation, to locate callers for outdoor 911 calls. Unfortunately, both technologies have limitations that make them less than suited when people cut the cord and use wireless calls to call 911. They are either not accurate enough, or they do not function at all. For example, GPS generally does not work well indoors.

However, fortunately, the transition to IP-based and network-based technologies is also spurring new investments in technologies that, while not originally designed for location determination such as in-building communication infrastructure, allows us to greatly improve the reliability and availability of location information. For example, Wi-Fi, Bluetooth beacons, and distributed antennae systems could be used to locate callers inside buildings.

To succeed in meeting the challenges and leverage the opportunities, all stakeholders must work together to ensure that every 911 call receives the appropriate response, that every American is alerted when danger is imminent, whether they use old technology or new technology.

Thank you.

[The prepared statement of Mr. Schulzrinne follows:]

PREPARED STATEMENT OF HENNING SCHULZRINNE, CHIEF TECHNOLOGY OFFICER, FEDERAL COMMUNICATIONS COMMISSION

Introduction

Chairman Pryor, Ranking Member Wicker, and Members of the Committee, I appreciate the opportunity to appear before you today to provide an overview of the technology transitions associated with migration to Internet Protocol ("IP") as well as the challenges and opportunities confronting us as we move forward through these transitions.

As you know, what we commonly refer to as the "IP transition" is not a single transition, but consists of multiple transitions all happening at the same time.

The elements of these technology transitions are a key concern of the Commission, with public safety as one of the fundamental values that need to be protected during the transition.

We are witnessing simultaneous transitions in three technology layers, with intertwining impacts:

1. At the application layer, voice services based on Time-Division Multiplexing (TDM) are rapidly moving to Voice-over-Internet Protocol (VoIP). This transition is occurring whether the network is wireless, where the technology is known as VoLTE, or for cable, fiber and copper networks. Technologically, the protocols used for these services are very similar.

2. At the network transport layer, TDM circuits served as the content-neutral conveyor of information. Internet Protocol packets are now replacing these circuits.

3. Finally, our core access networks were dominated by copper telephone wires, but are becoming much more diverse at the physical layer, with fiber, coaxial cable, wireless, and satellite added to the technology mix.

A much more diverse technological environment offers opportunities for advancing consumer welfare and public safety. For example, we can now bring IP connectivity to Public Safety Answering Points (PSAPs), the centers that handle the Nation's 911 calls, in many more ways than we were able to do before. But it also offers challenges in the sense that the technology is both more complicated and lacks some of the features that we previously relied upon as part of our public safety infrastructure.

Let me turn to some of the challenges that I believe we face going forward. The challenges are related in multiple ways and also have a generational component. Much of the legacy technology that underlies our existing telecommunication voice infrastructure was designed and built in the 1970s and 1980s. This infrastructure is rapidly aging, and we are also seeing generational turnover of the individuals that have designed, built and maintained that infrastructure.

Moreover, in the last few years, PSAPs and emergency management offices have had to deal with an increasing set of challenges, many induced by the technology changes described earlier. Some of these challenges include:

- Combatting Telephony Denial of Service (TDOS) attacks, where criminals try to extort money from employees of hospitals, schools and PSAPs, and, if that fails, barrage the organization with phone calls, typically with spoofed caller ID and originating abroad. These phone calls then prevent incoming calls from reaching the business line of PSAPs, for example.

- Delivering robust and reliable emergency alerts, such as Wireless Emergency Alerts (WEA) sent to mobile phones. These alerts provide crucial warnings to deal with imminent threats to life and property, *e.g.,* tornado warnings advising to "seek shelter now", but the alert systems are less well-suited to provide more extensive information or to support post-disaster recovery. Public safety officials seeking to provide more information to the public are often forced to improvise using cobbled-together technologies such as blogs, e-mail lists, and Twitter.

- Preventing outages of critical communications networks. VoIP-based systems and centralized ALI databases can support a large number of PSAPs with a very small number of servers. However, recent outages have illustrated that there is a risk of increased impact when these systems fail. Designing and testing such systems carefully to avoid single points of failure and to recover quickly remains an open challenge.

- Leveraging new technologies and services. For example, many Americans now expect to be able to reach public safety by text, not just voice call. People with hearing or speech disabilities cannot readily use voice 911; victims or witnesses of domestic abuse may fear that a voice call will place them in danger. While the four major national cellular operators have voluntarily agreed to make text-to-911 available nationwide earlier last month, relatively few PSAPs are ready to receive text messages.

- Even for traditional mobile voice 911 calls, determining the caller's location has become more challenging. As mandated by Commission rules, wireless providers need to deliver the caller's geographic location to the PSAP within specified accuracy bounds. However, the requirements were drafted when wireless phones were largely used while driving or outdoors. As has been reported extensively,[1] an increasing number of consumers no longer have traditional residential landlines. Also, emergency calls may be placed from work places, using the caller's own mobile device rather than a desk phone. It is estimated[2] that about 70 percent of all emergency calls are now originating on mobile phones, and 56 percent of those mobile calls are placed from indoor locations. The most common high-accuracy technology, GPS, generally does not work indoors due to signal attenuation, except in light-duty (wood frame) construction. Thus, new location technologies are needed. I will discuss some of the options later on.

Household Habits and Communication Resources are Changing

For many decades, emergency communication professionals could safely assume that households had a common set of communication resources: a landline phone, with the central office able to power the phone over the copper line to the home when commercial power to the home was disrupted; a television with an antenna, tuned to a relatively small number of local stations; and a transistor radio supporting both AM and FM, with the capability to run on battery power.

Newer households look very different: most likely, they won't have a landline phone and, if they do, the cable or fiber-to-the-home VoIP service is likely to only provide a few hours of standby service on a local battery if there is a power disruption. Today's houses may also not have a television or use it much less frequently,

---

[1] CDC, *Wireless Substitution: Early Release of Estimates From the National Health Interview Survey, July–December 2012;* at *http://www.cdc.gov/nchs/data/nhis/earlyrelease/wireless201 306.pdf.*

[2] See sources cited in *FCC Acts To Help Emergency Responders Locate Wireless 911 Callers,* February 21, 2014; at *http://www.fcc.gov/document/fcc-acts-help-emergency-responders-locate-wireless-911-callers*

relying on a laptop or tablet for watching video. Thus, Emergency Alert System (EAS) alerts broadcast via radio and television may not reach such households. The Internet, whether delivered via a home Wi-Fi network to a tablet or home PC or via a mobile wireless network to a smartphone, is often the primary means of keeping up with news and communicating with family and friends. These technologies may also rely on battery back-up options than are time-limited. For example, a smartphone battery may only sustain device operation for eight to 12 hours.

Emergency communication, in particular, has not always kept up with these changes. Many communities have set up automated "reverse 911" systems, but these typically only reach landlines. The Wireless Emergency Alert (WEA) system can only transmit 90 characters and cannot contain web links; thus, messages generally advise recipients to tune to local media—using a television set or radio that the household may not have. Communities seeking to convey information to their constituents often use commodity services, such as community mailing lists, Twitter feeds, Facebook pages, or local web pages to convey emergency-related information.

The development of IP-based networks may create opportunities to improve emergency communications. For example, agencies such as the Federal Emergency Management Agency (FEMA) could provide common, cloud-hosted emergency management systems to communities. Since Internet advertising is typically localized, the potential exists to provide emergency alerts via ad delivery networks that would complement EAS or Integrated Public Alert Warning System (IPAWS) alerts without requiring communities to make expensive technological upgrades.

Indirect 911

Currently, the most common way to reach the PSAP is by a human-initiated voice call. However, in the IP environment, other home safety devices, *e.g.*, network-connected smoke detectors, may provide alternative means of reaching emergency assistance. Currently, many alert monitoring services rely on operators in call centers to contact PSAPs. With NG911, there are opportunities for such monitoring services to convey much more information to the PSAP, but common standards and operational procedures are needed.

Technology Opportunities in all-IP networks

One of the most promising opportunities for IP-based emergency management networks is the ability to separate the provision of technology services from answering calls. Thus, instead of each PSAP or county provisioning their own NG911 services, they can share communication services, while deciding separately what the most efficient PSAP size is.

If emergency calls provide more information, it may also be much easier to prioritize calls, and recognize calls or messages that are reporting a known emergency, as often happens for fires or accidents.

Indoor Location

Probably the most immediate challenge for emergency calls is to maintain the location accuracy that has existed for 9–1–1 landline calls since the 1980s. As I noted earlier, as consumers have dropped landlines in favor of mobile devices, this capability is no longer assured. As the Commission recently acknowledged, people are making more wireless calls to 911 from indoors, and these calls are more difficult to locate. There are, however, new and promising indoor location technologies emerging. And the Commission is currently looking at new rules that would improve indoor location accuracy.

Conclusion

The technology transitions offer both unprecedented opportunities and challenges to emergency communication. As I have tried to illustrate, emergency services can leverage the new technologies to improve efficiency and effectiveness. I look forward to exploring many of these issues along with others to see how we can use the technology opportunities, not just those offered by classical emergency response and alerting technologies, but also by consumer technologies to make everybody safer, make public safety more efficient, and ensure networks are responsive to both the cultural and technology changes that our citizenry is undergoing.

Thank you very much.

Senator PRYOR. Thank you.
Mr. Banks?

STATEMENT OF JONATHAN BANKS, SENIOR VICE PRESIDENT, LAW AND POLICY, UNITED STATES TELECOM ASSOCIATION (USTELECOM)

Mr. BANKS. Good morning. Good morning, Chairman Pryor, Ranking Member Wicker, and the members of the Subcommittee.

My name is Jonathan Banks, and I am the Senior Vice President for Law and Policy at USTelecom. Thank you for holding this hearing.

USTelecom represents broadband companies, ranging from some of the largest companies in the U.S. to some of the smallest co-operatives and family owned telecom providers in rural America. They serve some of the most rural areas in the country, as well as the most urban, and use a broad range of technologies, including broadband and Internet protocol, to do so.

To begin, I would like to note the recent tragedy caused by an extremely powerful tornado touching down in Arkansas, north of Little Rock, in late April. The tornado caused substantial loss of life and damage. Communication services were affected, with poles blown down, cables severed, facilities damaged, and cell towers destroyed.

One local carrier, Windstream, was somehow able to keep a switch up and running in a building that lost its walls to the tornado's winds and suffered substantial rain damage. This storm illustrates that no network is or can be 100 percent reliable, but a well-coordinated response in Arkansas got networks up and running relatively quickly.

Careful preparation for emergencies can make a huge difference in the effect that disasters have on communications networks and the customers they serve. Our industry has long participated in emergency readiness planning with Government partners, and we will continue to do so.

The transition to modern broadband networks and IP services promises enormous benefits to our country. The FCC's National Broadband Plan says that building these networks is the great infrastructure challenge of our time. The communications industry is stepping up to the plate, investing about $685 billion over the last decade in infrastructure, with about $70 billion of that being invested just last year.

We agree that as we navigate through this transition, that there are key values that cannot be left behind. FCC Chairman Wheeler describes these values as making up a network compact between communications providers and the public. Network reliability and public safety are essential elements of this compact, and they are key values of our industry.

Our industry has a long history of working with Federal and State governments, public utility commissions, the public safety community, and industry standards bodies on these issues. We have been working with these partners to understand the transition to broadband and IP services for well over a decade. I provide a brief summary of some of these efforts in my written testimony.

In closing, I would like to reiterate our commitment to working with this committee and our full range of partners to ensure that the promise of broadband connectivity and the power of IP services

9

deliver to consumers the safe and secure networks and robust capabilities that will empower them for the 21st century.

Thank you.

[The prepared statement of Mr. Banks follows:]

PREPARED STATEMENT OF JONATHAN BANKS, SENIOR VICE PRESIDENT, LAW AND POLICY, UNITED STATES TELECOM ASSOCIATION (USTELECOM)

Chairman Pryor, Ranking Member Wicker, and Members of the Subcommittee:

Thank you for the opportunity to testify on this important topic. My name is Jon Banks, and I serve as Senior Vice President of Law and Policy at the United States Telecom Association. USTelecom represents innovative broadband companies ranging from some of the largest companies in the U.S. economy to some of the smallest cooperatives and family-owned telecom providers in rural America. Our members offer a wide range of communications services on both a fixed and mobile basis, and the overwhelming majority of them offer advanced broadband services including voice, video, and data. They serve some of the most rural areas in the country as well as the most urban and use a broad range of technologies, including Internet Protocol, to do so. The customers that rely on our networks include consumers, businesses large and small, and government entities at the local, state, and Federal levels. Of particular importance given the topic of this hearing, they include first responders and Public Safety Answering Points.

Our industry has long recognized that a safe and secure communications network is vital to public safety and to our Nation's prosperity. We have spent decades building and maintaining that network and working with the public safety community and our government partners to ensure that first responders and other officials can communicate during natural or man-made disasters, and that consumers can call for help during an emergency. From the 1960s and 1970s when 911 services began to be provided through the deployment of upgraded E911 services and Next Generation 911, we have worked to deliver reliable service. Our member companies' commitment to providing highly reliable service to our customers throughout the country and to working with the public safety community, our government partners, and industry standards bodies remains undiminished as the country moves to newer, more modern communications networks. In fact, the transition to these newer, more modern broadband networks holds great promise for improved emergency communications and services as well as more robust and reliable networks.

Much has changed since the early days of making 911 a reality. Over the last decade, communications companies have been investment leaders in our country, putting over $671 billion dollars to work in building and upgrading communications infrastructure. The wireline industry alone invested $278 billion over this period, accounting for about 41 percent of total investment, with the remainder made up by investments in wireless and cable infrastructure. And this level of investment is continuing. USTelecom estimates that investment in broadband and IP communications infrastructure very likely exceeded $70 billion in 2013, surpassing the average level of investment of about $66 billion annually over the last decade.

The result of this continuing huge investment is that consumers and businesses today have multiple new broadband networks available to them that are far more robust than the old telephone network. Building these broadband networks—fixed and mobile—is the great infrastructure challenge of our time. As the National Broadband Plan notes, meeting this challenge can produce enormous benefits:

> Broadband is a foundation for economic growth, job creation, global competitiveness and a better way of life. It is enabling entire new industries and unlocking vast new possibilities for existing ones. It is changing how we educate children, deliver health care, manage energy, ensure public safety, engage government, and access, organize and disseminate knowledge.[1]

By continuing to invest on this massive scale, the industry has made great strides in meeting this infrastructure challenge. Today, over 99 percent of Americans have access to broadband service at the FCC defined capacity of 4 Mbps downstream and 1 Mbps upstream. Ninety-two percent of the population has access to robust wireline infrastructure with 88 percent of the population having access to two or more wired networks. Ninety-nine percent have access to mobile service and 90 percent have access to 4 or more separate mobile networks. Our members are working to build and operate Gigabit and fiber-to-the home networks in urban and rural

---

[1] *National Broadband Plan* at XI.

areas across the country. Cable systems are upgrading their networks to provide faster service. Fast LTE mobile networks are also growing quickly, providing more alternatives for consumers.

Removing obstacles to broadband deployment will help drive this process, and the White House has engaged industry on examining barriers to deployment across federally owned and managed land. Another way to incent additional investment would be to remove outdated regulations on traditional phone companies. These regulations "require certain carriers to maintain POTS [plain old telephone service]—a requirement that is not sustainable—and lead to investments in assets that could be stranded," and divert investment away from new networks and new services.[2]

Ensuring that broadband and mobile networks reach everywhere throughout our country is a goal we must continually strive to meet. In the most rural areas of our country, this will require governmental support because there is no private business case that can support building and operating broadband networks in these areas. The FCC's universal service program can play an essential role here, as can state programs that support communications infrastructure. Our industry continues to work to ensure that universal service programs continue to support the delivery of robust communications services in high cost areas of our country in the most efficient and effective way possible.

One result of all this investment in newer, more modern technologies is consumers have been choosing newer broadband and mobile technologies because they offer a plethora of options that were not previously available to meet consumers' communications needs. USTelecom projects that, by the end of this year, only one-quarter of the households in the country will continue to be served by traditional phone service. In some states this number may be as low as 15 percent of households remaining on that traditional network. By the end of this year, about 45 percent of households will have chosen to drop traditional phone service entirely, choosing instead to rely on mobile service for their voice needs, both inside and outside the home. According to the Centers for Disease Control, in many states over 50 percent of households have already cut the cord and chosen to rely on mobile service. The remaining 30 percent of households will have chosen from among a range of newer Voice over Internet Protocol services, often delivered by cable companies, for their voice needs at home. Of course, many households will choose to have both wireless and wired options available for calling. About 89 percent of households have at least one wireless phone, allowing multiple options for communications. Only about 9 percent of households are dependent solely on a wired option for calling.

This transition to broadband networks and IP services is well underway today as consumers and businesses continue to make choices among a range of competitive communications options. The transition to broadband and IP services is not an "if" phenomenon—much of it has happened—but a question of how to best manage the transition. And, in particular, how to ensure that public safety and network reliability are preserved and that we leverage the unique capabilities of broadband and IP to deliver 21st century public safety services. For example, making the added functionality of next generation 911 available to allow pictures and video to be delivered to PSAPs and first responders could significantly improve public safety. Our industry looks forward to working with the public safety community and governmental entities to make NG911 a reality. And for consumers, voice communication is obviously not the only functionality that the IP transition enables. For example, when it comes to public safety and health care benefits, more and more senior citizens, people with disabilities, and medical patients living in rural America are benefiting from technologies such as home health monitoring and other health-related applications.

Fortunately, the communications industry has seen other important technology transitions all the way through that can provide models for ensuring the IP transition leaves no one behind. In 2002, for example, the transition from analog to digital mobile service was well underway from a consumer perspective. That year, the FCC concluded that its mandate that carriers continue to provide an analog signal in addition to a digital signal was no longer necessary to achieve national coverage and incent competition. Further, the FCC found that the analog mandate was imposing unnecessary costs on carriers and hindering the efficient use of spectrum. Thus, the FCC scheduled an end for the analog mandate setting February 18, 2008, as the date at which carriers could move to providing solely digital service. In the interim period, the FCC worked with carriers and specific populations that could have been adversely affected by the transition to ensure that no one was left behind.

---

[2] *Id.* at 59.

Planning for the transition to IP networks has been going on within communications companies for quite some time and with our government partners as well. Much of this planning has focused on network safety and security issues. For example, the President's National Security Telecommunications Advisory Committee (NSTAC), which provides the President with a unique source of national security and emergency preparedness communications policy expertise from leaders in the communications industry, has been examining and reporting on security and reliability issues involved in the transition to IP and broadband networks since at least 1999. In 2005, the NSTAC noted that the convergence of wireless, wireline, and Internet Protocol (IP) networks is causing a shift in the way that governments and critical infrastructures will meet their needs for national security and emergency preparedness communications today and in the future. The NSTAC has examined a broad range of infrastructure, security and operational vulnerabilities stemming from network convergence and its task forces have provided recommendations to mitigate the vulnerabilities. USTelecom and its members have been an integral part of NSTAC and will continue to work within the Committee to ensure that public safety remains a priority during the IP Transition.

Our members also continue to work closely with the Department of Homeland Security through, for example, the Communications Sector Coordination Council and the Critical Infrastructure Partnership Advisory Council, on network security and reliability issues and the transition to IP networks. A concise review of some of these activities can be found in the Critical Infrastructure Partnership Advisory Council's 2013 Annual Report.

In addition, USTelecom has long been active with the FCC in this area. Chairman Wheeler has often mentioned the importance of public safety and security to the compact between providers of voice service and their customers and the need for the FCC to ensure that key values like these are properly imported into the IP and broadband world. We agree. In response to Congress's directive that the agency develop a National Broadband Plan that would "ensure that all people of the United States have access to broadband capability," the FCC put together an extremely valuable roadmap to an IP and broadband future. The Plan explains that "broadband can bolster efforts to improve public safety and homeland security by allowing first responders to send and receive video and data, by ensuring all Americans can access emergency services and improving the way Americans are notified about emergencies."[3] We remain committed to working with the FCC on the implementation of these recommendations.

The FCC's Communications Security, Reliability and Interoperability Council (CSRIC) has played, and will continue to play, an important role in planning for a seamless transition. CSRIC working groups comprised of knowledgeable industry participants have produced a broad range of reports and recommendations covering key topics on emergency preparedness, network reliability and network security. The FCC recently convened a new CSRIC industry working group to examine and report on the powering of customer premises equipment such as telephone handsets given the growing consumer preference for VoIP service. VoIP networks generally do not benefit from network powering available through traditional phone networks, instead relying on commercial power and battery back-up. The working group intends to recommend outreach and communications strategies for increasing consumer awareness of back-up power needs and developing best practices for powering consumer devices during commercial power failures.

Finally, a number of standards-setting bodies are also engaged in planning for the IP transition. Indeed, the transition ties together much of the work done by one of our industry's leading standards bodies, the Alliance for Telecommunications Industry Solutions, or ATIS. Specific to the subject of this hearing, for example, ATIS has convened a task force to examine the IP transition's potential effect on important public safety applications such as alarm circuits to local fire and police departments and circuits that monitor railroad crossings.

USTelecom and our members believe that our Nation's 21st century networks should provide 21st century public safety solutions. We look forward to working with this subcommittee, our full range of governmental partners including the White House, the Federal Communications Commission, Department of Commerce, Department of Homeland Security, state and local governments and public utility commissions, the public safety community (including APCO and NENA), and industry standards bodies to ensure that the promise of broadband connectivity and the power of IP services deliver to consumers the safe and secure networks and robust capabilities that will empower them for the 21st century.

---

[3] *Id.* at XIV.

Senator PRYOR. Thank you.
Ms. Griffin?

STATEMENT OF JODIE GRIFFIN, SENIOR STAFF ATTORNEY, PUBLIC KNOWLEDGE

Ms. GRIFFIN. Chairman Pryor, Ranking Member Wicker, and members of the Subcommittee, thank you for inviting me to testify today.

My name is Jodie Griffin, and I am a Senior Staff Attorney at Public Knowledge, an organization that advocates for the public's access to knowledge and open communications platforms.

The phone network transition presents tremendous potential advantages for our Nation, but we need to make sure these transitions result in a meaningful step forward for every person who depends on the network. Americans trust the protections of the phone network. We conduct our business and personal communications, assuming that the phone network will just work because it always has.

During emergencies, we can call for help from police, firefighters, and hospitals. In the rare instance that any part of the system breaks down, local, State, and Federal authorities intervene as if our lives depend on it, because they do.

In January, in a unanimous bipartisan vote, the Federal Communications Commission recognized that our phone network policies must serve certain basic, enduring values: public safety and national security, universal access, competition, and consumer protection. Our policies in the network transition must serve all of these values.

This hearing focuses on public safety and reliability, but a conversation about these values will always entail the rest of the network compact. After all, when you need to make an emergency call, what you really need is a reliable network to make that call. A person can't call 911 if she doesn't have phone service in the first place, and if she lives in a rural area, she may waste precious time trying to get connected.

New technologies have great promise, but they don't always meet the critical needs for a reliable telecommunications network. We have already seen reports of wireless carriers providing insufficient location data to public safety answering points, or in the event of a power outage, fiber-based services will require battery back-up, unlike traditional self-powered copper lines, and wireless services will be useless if the cell towers also lose power.

Public safety services and reliability are so firmly ingrained in our network now, many consumers may simply assume new technologies will give them the same guarantees they have in the existing network. If, for example, a customer doesn't realize his fiber-based service needs battery back-up until the power has already gone out, he can't prepare for a prolonged outage.

It is critical to ensure the FCC has the authority it needs to preserve the network compact and serve its fundamental values. In light of the recent Net Neutrality ruling from the D.C. Circuit, policymakers must make sure the FCC can implement rules to require carriers to complete calls and provide basic service, even after the network has moved to IP, or wireless or fiber infrastructure.

To be clear, no one is suggesting we should hold back on technology. The question is how to make this technology work for all of the 300 million people who rely on our network every day. The underlying technology may be changing, but the essential services and consumers' expectations for them remain the same, and our national policies must reflect that fact.

Thank you, and I look forward to your questions.

[The prepared statement of Ms. Jodie Griffin follows:]

PREPARED STATEMENT OF JODIE GRIFFIN, SENIOR STAFF ATTORNEY, PUBLIC KNOWLEDGE

Chairman Pryor, Ranking Member Wicker, and Members of the Subcommittee, thank you for this opportunity to discuss the IP transition, public safety, and network reliability. My name is Jodie Griffin and I am a Senior Staff Attorney at Public Knowledge, a nonprofit public interest organization that promotes the public's access to information and culture through open, competitive, universally accessible, and affordable communications networks.

Introduction

The transition of our wireline networks to Internet Protocol (IP)-based services is a tremendous opportunity for our nation, but we must make sure the transition results in an actual upgrade in technology without a downgrade in the services upon which Americans depend. We are now in the midst of the transition: carriers are already actively moving their networks from the traditional Time-Division Multiplexing (TDM) protocol to IP-based technology, and from copper infrastructure to wireless service or fiber. The Federal Communications Commission (FCC) has responded to these technological shifts by collecting public comments, initiating a series of trials, and beginning the process of forming a new framework to handle the policy questions raised by these transitions.

In the network transition, the stakes are high, and it is critical for policymakers to ensure that everyone continues to have access to a reliable network for personal, business, and emergency communications. In addition to bringing new opportunities, the phone network transition presents risks, including concerns the new networks will lack important features that consumers have counted on for decades. This means policymakers at all levels of government must ensure the transition is handled responsibly and everyday Americans are better off as a result of the transition.

The phone network in the U.S. has quietly and reliably provided benefits to the American public for over 100 years. These benefits have become so firmly ingrained in the U.S. economy, public safety systems, and personal communications that users take for granted the policies that make them possible. These benefits were not a happy accident—they were the result of deliberate communications policies that demanded a telecommunications network that served its users first and foremost.

One of the things we've come to love about our phone network is the ability to conduct our business and personal communications as if we can always trust that the network will just work—because it will. We can choose the type of phone we use. When the power goes out during a natural disaster, our phones—and the central offices that service them—will keep working. In times of emergency, we can always call for aid from police, firefighters, and medical teams. When someone calls a friend that call will always go through—regardless of which carriers the two users subscribe to or where they each live. When the bill comes for that call, the user can rest assured that there will be no fraudulent charges and the carrier will not have "traded" her to another carrier without her permission. If a user changes phone companies, she can keep her phone number. We know that we can benefit from the innovations and features built on the phone network because it is an open platform: innovations like the Internet, new handsets, calling cards, and collect calls all arose because of the network's openness. And in the rare instance that any part of this system breaks down, we know that there are government authorities at the local, state, and Federal levels equipped to fix the problem and protect users' interests.

Every single one of these benefits is the result of deliberate policy choices that served specific basic values. Our phone network became the unparalleled success we know today because our policymakers valued five fundamental principles: (1) service to all Americans; (2) competition and interconnection; (3) consumer protection; (4)

network reliability; and (5) public safety.[1] These values are no less relevant and, if anything, are even more important as we begin the transition to the next iteration of our Nation's communications networks.

As we move forward in the network transition, we cannot step back from the basic commitments that have protected consumers and promoted affordable communications service for decades. We must ensure the next generation of our communications networks are a true step forward for everyone and no one is left worse off as a result of the transition.

Basic Voice Service is Still Important

Even as we move to new technologies that bring exciting new opportunities for customers to access the Internet and other IP-based services, it is important to remember that basic voice service is still vital to public safety as well as the day-to-day personal and business communications of millions of people across the Nation. This means our national policies should be shaped with a mind toward preserving the protections and benefits people currently rely on while encouraging new opportunities for better or more efficient service.

It is important to note that 96 percent of U.S. residents subscribe to some kind of telephone service.[2] Of those, over 100 million people rely on traditional copper POTS (Plain Old Telephone Service). 5 percent of the country relies exclusively on POTS—that's 15 million people who rely *solely* on traditional phone service.[3] Which, incidentally, means the remaining 85 million people subscribing to POTS do so despite also having a mobile phone or other voice product. We can safely assume those 85 million people do not simply enjoy writing two checks each month. Rather, traditional phone service must offer those users something that newer technologies currently do not.

Unfortunately, we are already seeing complaints arise across the country that indicate the network compact may start fraying at the edges if policymakers don't step in to protect consumers. As Public Knowledge, The Utility Reform Network, and several other state consumer advocates and public interest groups have noted, reports have surfaced across the country indicating carriers are forcing customers off of traditional copper-based phone service.[4] Complaints from customers in California, Maryland, New York, New Jersey, Illinois, and the District of Columbia have stated that they are being involuntarily moved to fiber or IP-based service (or some combination thereof), even if those new technologies fail to serve all of the users' needs or will be more expensive. What's more, this may only be the tip of the iceberg. After all, in deregulated states where the utilities commissions have no authority over quality of service or pricing for basic service, state-level authorities may not be able to even collect data from customer complaints.

We have also already seen complaints from rural residents experiencing degraded service due to rural call completion problems. As I will discuss below, the IP transition can create unexpected problems in rural customers' service even without any parties necessarily acting in bad faith. This is exactly why the FCC must continue to have authority to handle unanticipated problems and ensure customers continue to have reliable service.[5] Finally, the FCC's Wireline Competition Bureau recently found that the average rate for basic voice service in urban areas is $20.46, indicating that even basic service is not as inexpensive as some may have assumed.

Added together, these issues raise the serious question of whether all customers are indeed moving to new services out of a genuine desire to change, or if at least some have been moved off the copper network due to service degradation, increased fees, or through no choice of their own at all. If a carrier is letting its copper network degrade or is telling customers they must move to fiber or wireless service in violation of its common carrier obligations, can we really call that a fair market choice on the part of the customer? And even in the cases where the customer has

---

[1] *See* Jodie Griffin and Harold Feld, *Five Fundamentals for the Phone Network Transition,* Public Knowledge (July 2013).

[2] *Universal Service Monitoring Report,* Wireline Competition Bureau, FCC, at 41, Table 3.1 (Oct. 2013), available at *http://transition.fcc.gov/Bureaus/Common_Carrier/Reports/FCC-State_Link/Monitor/2013_Monitoring_Report.pdf.*

[3] Anna-Maria Kovacs, *Telecommunications Competition: The Infrastructure-Investment Race,* Internet Innovation Alliance (Oct. 2013), *http://internetinnovation.org/images/misc_content/study-telecommunications-competition-09072013.pdf.*

[4] Letter from Jodie Griffin, Senior Staff Attorney, Public Knowledge, *et al.* to Julie A. Veach, Chief, Wireline Competition Bureau, FCC (May 12, 2014), available at *http://www.publicknowledge.org/assets/uploads/blog/14.05.12_Copper_Letter.pdf.*

[5] To that end, the Public Safety and Economic Security Communications Act is an important step forward in protecting rural customers relying on a dependable phone network. *See* Public Safety and Economic Security Communications Act of 2014, S. 2125, 113th Cong. (2014), available at *https://www.govtrack.us/congress/bills/113/s2125/text.*

a meaningful choice to move to services using newer technologies, it is hard to accept the notion that customer actually *wants* the new service to have less reliability, more expensive power backup options, or less accurate 911 location data. When it comes to network reliability and public safety, these are not compromises we should be asking customers to make.

The Network's Fundamental Values

This past January, the FCC, unanimously and with bipartisan support, recognized the fundamental network compact that has successfully guided communications policy for decades.[6] That compact preserves certain enduring values that ensure our communications networks will remain the envy of the world as we move into IP-based services and new physical infrastructure.

The policies that guide the network transition should serve certain proven fundamental values and continue to protect consumers and encourage innovation. These fundamental values—public safety and national security, universal access, competition, and consumer protection—capture the basic principles that made our phone network a resounding success and can do the same for the next generation of communications technology.

Public Safety and National Security

It is unquestioned that when someone calls 911, that person needs to know beyond a shadow of a doubt that she will be connected in one second. Everyday Americans rely on 911 daily to call for help in time of need. The FCC has already begun to look to the future of public safety requirements with the Next Generation 911 transition.[7] This conversation, however, is also best situated in the broader context of the overall PSTN transition, both to evaluate the effect of 911 proposals on other aspects of the network, and to anticipate the impact of non-911 proposals on our emergency communications systems.

The network transition can bring with it new opportunities to expand emergency services. For example, the recent deployment of text-to-911 capabilities in certain areas can help people seek emergency aid when placing a voice call is not feasible.[8] However, we cannot simply assume that new technologies will continue to support the 911 features people rely on after the transition. In particular, as customers increasingly place 911 calls on wireless devices, policymakers should ensure carriers provide emergency responders with detailed and accurate location data. The California Chapter of the National Emergency Number Association has reported a recent significant decrease in the percentage of wireless 911 calls delivering more detailed Phase II location data to public safety answering points (PSAPs).[9] If PSAPs do not receive adequate location data from carriers, they cannot find callers asking for help unless the caller can describe her own location, which may be difficult in certain emergency situations and places an extra burden on anyone who has a communication disability or additional language barrier. Elsewhere, AT&T's Wireless Home Phone product—marketed as a replacement for traditional landline phone service—tells customers in the fine print they will be required to give 911 operators their address, rather than have their location information transmitted to PSAPs automatically.[10] But it doesn't have to be this way. The technology transitions offer opportunities to integrate multiple location technologies to give more specific loca-

---

[6] *See Technology Transitions,* GN Docket No. 13–5, *AT&T Petition to Launch a Proceeding Concerning the TDM-to-IP Transition,* GN Docket No. 12–353, *Connect America Fund,* WC Docket No. 10–90, *Structure and Practices of the Video Relay Service Program,* CG Docket No. 10–51, *Telecommunications Relay Services and Speech-to-Speech Services for Individuals with Hearing and Speech Disabilities,* CG Docket No. 03–123, *Numbering Policies for Modern Communications,* WC Docket No. 13–97, Order, Report and Order and Further Notice of Proposed Rulemaking, Report and Order, Order and Further Notice of Proposed Rulemaking, Proposal for Ongoing Data Initiative at ¶¶ 37–69 (rel. Jan. 31, 2014).

[7] The FCC is also working with surer authority in this area compared to other aspects of the PSTN transition, based on the Next Generation 911 Act. See Middle Class Tax Relief and Job Creation Act of 2012, Pub. L. No. 112–96 (2012), Title VI, Subtitle E.

[8] *See What You Need to Know About Text-to-911,* FCC (May 23, 2014), *https://www.fcc.gov/text-to-911.*

[9] Letter from Danita L. Crombach, CALNENA, to Mignon Clyburn, Chairwoman, FCC (Aug. 12, 2013), *http://www.calnena.org/communications/To-FCC–08–12–2013/CALNENA-Letter-to-FCC–081213.pdf.*

[10] AT&T Wireless Home Phone & Internet, *http://www.att.com/shop/wireless/devices/att/wireless-home-phone-and-internet-black.html* (last visited June 2, 2014).

tion information and to find more efficient ways to notify emergency services when help is needed.[11]

Public safety rules must ensure emergency services like 911 and geolocation technologies continue to help first responders offer emergency care, regardless of whether the network the customer uses is wireless or wireline, copper or fiber. The conversion to an all-IP network offers an opportunity to further facilitate emergency communications, and that opportunity must not be squandered. This also includes ensuring that the thousands of alarm systems and alarm system standards that rely on access to a "telephone line" are not disrupted by the transition, as we have seen them be disrupted by the attempted transition to Voice Link in Fire Island, New York.[12]

When the traditional architecture of the PSTN no longer exists, it is crucial that consumers are able to contact emergency services when they need it most. The moments in which the public relies upon emergency services like 911 are literally life-or-death, and it is crucial that policymakers implement rules that maintain the public safety components of the phone network. To its credit, the FCC has already begun the process of creating a framework for Next Generation 911 services, but these issues must also be considered in the broader context of the overall shift of the PSTN to new technologies.

Network Reliability

The basic mechanisms of the network must continue to function throughout and after the PSTN transition, even and especially in emergency situations. Above all else, Americans rely on their communications networks to work consistently and reliably. Above all else, a successful transition means that phone numbers still work and calls still go through with the same reliability they do today.

One important part of making sure the phone network just continues to *work* on a day-to-day basis is ensuring the network's numbering system continues to function throughout and after the transition. Contrary to the beliefs of some, what defines the "public switched network" is not its underlying technology, but rather its use of phone numbers under the North American Numbering Plan.[13] Fortunately, the FCC has recognized the importance of ensuring the continuing functionality and security of our numbering system, and has included a phone numbering testbed among its initiatives to more fully understand the transition. The FCC should use the lessons it learns in this testbed to determine the requirements for future Local Number Portability Administrators (LNPAs) and to ensure smooth transitions between administrators when they occur. The FCC could also use this opportunity to consider authorizing multiple LNPAs under §251(e), given the increasing ease of coordinating data between multiple databases.[14]

The FCC currently exercises its authority over phone numbers to distribute phone numbers through the North American Numbering Plan (NANP). This raises the stark and critical question: who will be able to obtain numbers when all carriers have transitioned to IP-based technology? How will phone numbers work in a world with no TDM-based PSTN? These are questions that we absolutely must answer if the phone network as users now know it is to continue operating post-transition.

After the transition, there will also be no "copper safety net" to offer the reliability that users have come to expect with basic phone service. Nevertheless, users' phone service—regardless of the protocols or materials it uses—must be able to withstand emergency situations. Even now we are still witnessing phone network technology "upgrades" result in less redundancy and backup power in the system and increased reliance on the commercial power grid, creating a single point of failure when disaster strikes and users need to communicate most.

The FCC's Wireline Competition Bureau has acknowledged that policymakers must be mindful of the network transition's impact on reliability and performance during power outages, even when the network is transitioning to a technology like fiber that it commonly considered to be an improvement over copper networks.[15] Fiber offers the potential for faster data speeds and more network capacity, but, unlike the traditional copper network, is not self-powered and needs battery backup

[11] *See* Henning Schulzrinne, *Public Safety Communications in a Time of Transition,* FCC (Apr. 17, 2014), *http://transition.fcc.gov/bureaus/pshs/docs/2014-PublicSafetyWorkshop.pdf.*
[12] *See* Jodie Griffin, *The Phone Network Transition: Lessons from Fire Island,* Public Knowledge (Mar. 7, 2014), *http://www.publicknowledge.org/news-blog/blogs/the-phone-network-transition-lessons-from-fire-island.*
[13] 47 C.F.R. §20.3.
[14] 47 U.S.C. §251(e).
[15] *See* Julie Veach, Chief, Wireline Competition Bureau, *Protecting Consumers in the Transition from Copper Networks,* FCC Blog (May 7, 2014), *http://www.fcc.gov/blog/protecting-consumers-transition-copper-networks.*

17

during power outages. Similarly, fixed wireless services require batteries, and the battery backup for AT&T's Wireless Home Phone product, for example, only offers 1.5 hours of talk time and 18 hours of standby time.[16] As many communities that have experience hurricanes, tornadoes, and other natural disasters can attest, commercial power can be down for much longer than 18 hours, but users' need to have access to reliable communications remain unchanged.

This is not to say that we must reject any technology that is not self-powered, but we must ensure the network continues to be as reliable as possible during power outages while minimizing the burden on consumers to make it so. And where a new technology differs from the network customers have come to rely on, we must make those differences clear to customers so they are not caught unawares after the power has already gone out. We can recognize consumers' justified expectations based on the traditional network they've known for decades and pursue policies to meet those needs without demanding that technological change be stopped in its tracks.

As the PSTN continues its transition, the FCC and other policymakers must determine how they can ensure the post-transition PSTN continues to guarantee robust service for everyday uses and for emergency circumstances, when users need communications services most.

Universal Access

Issues of public safety and network reliability also raise the question: what *is* the basic service we're aiming to give everyone access to? This transition is an opportunity to look forward: what new opportunities are made possible by new technology, and how does that impact what we determine to be the "basic service" that all should have access to? The Communications Act specifies that universal service encompasses "an evolving level of telecommunications services" and that the FCC should take into account "advances in telecommunications and information technologies and services" as it decides what universal service will look like for homes, schools, libraries, and health care providers across the country.[17] Access to basic communications services reaps tremendous social and economic benefits to users, regardless of the material or technology used to transport the communications.

We cannot simply sit back and assume that new technologies will continue to reach everyone at affordable prices on their own. Even now, we see indications that the transition could result in customers losing access to wireline service—or indeed, any service at all—and having to pay more for services that might not even offer all of the features and reliability of the existing network. For example, AT&T is currently seeking FCC approval of a wire center trial proposal that offers no plan for serving 4 percent of the population at all in one of the trial areas.[18] AT&T's trial proposal also puts forward a plan to offer only a wireless product to a substantial percentage of the population, even though that wireless service currently cannot support features like medical alerts, alarm monitoring, credit card processing, 800 number service, dial-around calls, collect calls, elevator phone service, and E–911.[19] Technological transitions in the network should be a step forward for everyone—we cannot allow everyday networks users to fall through the cracks in a process that is supposed to *help* people obtain better affordable access to communications platforms.

Policymakers should also consider the impact of the phone network transition on the availability and affordability of Internet access. For example, the Wireless Home Phone and Internet product that AT&T currently offers costs $80.00 for unlimited calling and just 10 GB of data (the package is $140.00 for voice and 30 GB of data).[20] Under these plans, customers do not have the option of purchasing standalone broadband, so the least expensive package that includes broadband would be $80.00 for a mere 10 GB of usage. As a comparison, AT&T offers wireline Internet access over its DSL infrastructure for $14.95 for 150 GB of data.

One of the most important goals of communications policy in the United States is reaching universal service for all Americans across the country. The transition of

[16] AT&T Wireless Home Phone & Internet, *http://www.att.com/shop/wireless/devices/att/wireless-home-phone-and-internet-black.html* (last visited June 2, 2014).
[17] 47 U.S.C. § 254(c).
[18] AT&T Proposal for Wire Center Trials, *Technology Transitions,* GN Docket No. 13–5, *AT&T Petition to Launch a Proceeding Concerning the TDM-to-IP Transition,* GN Docket No. 12–353, at 14 (Feb. 27, 2014).
[19] AT&T Proposal for Wire Center Trials, Wire Center Trial Operating Plan, *Technology Transitions,* GN Docket No. 13–5, *AT&T Petition to Launch a Proceeding Concerning the TDM-to-IP Transition,* GN Docket No. 12–353, at 14–15 (Feb. 27, 2014).
[20] AT&T Wireless Home Phone & Internet, *http://www.att.com/shop/wireless/devices/att/wireless-home-phone-and-internet-black.html* (last visited June 2, 2014).

the PSTN is an opportunity to expand and improve the communications service that all Americans receive, and our communications authorities must determine how they can continue to serve that goal as the traditional make-up of the PSTN changes.

Competition

Interconnection and other competition policies lie at the heart of the development of a robust and competitive communications network. As we saw more than 100 years ago, without mandatory interconnection the phone network will slide inevitably toward monopoly as the largest carriers can gain anticompetitive advantages by withholding access to their customers from competitors. As carriers now move toward all-IP networks, policymakers must determine how they will ensure interconnection and competition among providers post-transition. These policies are critical to creating and maintaining a functioning interconnected network and a competitive market for communications services.

For example, subscribers to different networks must not find themselves with dropped calls or degraded quality of service due to "peering disputes" between carriers. If NBC and AT&T have a retransmission dispute and AT&T video subscribers temporarily lose NBC programs, it is annoying. But if Comcast and AT&T have a "peering dispute" and millions of AT&T wireless customers cannot reliably call Comcast landlines, it is a disaster. It is not enough to speculate that incentives will prevent such a thing from occurring. Policymakers must make sure such an event continues to be *impossible* after the transition.

The phone network transition also calls into question the future of other rules and policies designed to encourage competition among communications providers. For example, local number portability (LNP) obligations have currently been extended to VoIP providers so that VoIP customers may keep their North American Numbering Plan (NANP) telephone number when changing providers. LNP rules encourage competition by allowing consumers to respond to providers' price and service changes without losing their phone numbers. But at this juncture the questions inevitably arises: when the traditional PSTN is gone, what will happen to the NANP? How can LNP rules extend to all phone service providers without revisiting the foundation of the NANP or classifying VoIP service?

As the PSTN transitions to new physical facilities and IP protocols, it is critical to the competitive future of the market that the law and rules ensure carriers will continue to interconnect and rules will continue to promote competition in the marketplace to the benefit of consumers.

Consumer Protection

When we talk about a system that everyday Americans count on to call 911, businesses, and loved ones, we cannot ignore users' need for consumer protections in the network. Competition is important, but it does not always guarantee consumer protection. From the privacy of phone calls to truth-in-billing to slamming and cramming, Americans rely on a safety net of rules that protect them when they communicate with one another. Throughout and after the PSTN transition, consumers must continue to be adequately protected—including effective recourse through the timely resolution of complaints.

But on the Federal level, the Federal Communications Commission has only extended privacy rules to interconnected VoIP services by reasoning that those VoIP services send calls to and receive calls from the traditional phone network.[21] Customers should be able to rely on the same protections they have always enjoyed when they switch to what by all appearances seems like a pure replacement for "regular telephone" service. After the DC Circuit's recent decision in *Verizon* v. *FCC,* we can be more confident that the FCC could use its section 706 authority to continue consumer protections in the IP world, but Congress should continue to monitor movements in this space and ensure important consumer protection rules are actually carried over onto IP-based networks.

As the PSTN begins to transition to IP protocols and other upgraded technologies, policymakers must come to terms with how they will continue to protect consumers post-transition. All signs indicate that consumer protection rules will be equally, if not more, important post-transition than they are today, and if anything consumer protection agencies will need flexibility to ensure that current and future consumer protection rules serve the same basic social needs as they do today.

---

[21] 47 U.S.C. § 222.

19

The IP Transition and Rural Communities

The new pattern of carriers eager to replace existing networks with new, untested technologies after natural disasters or when wireline networks have simply been allowed to degrade will have especially strong consequences for rural communities. Rural areas depend on wireline services more than most, especially because wireless deployment—even beyond its general limitations compared to wireline service—is not very strong in rural areas. And when a rural community loses a wireline service provider that offered DSL or other broadband service, there is rarely any competing service to turn to for continued Internet access. At the very least, the rural farmers who grow our food should know that they will be able to make phone calls and access the Internet when needed to check weather patterns, predict crop growth, and make business arrangements to harvest and transport crops. This also impacts more than just rural communities themselves—when farmers are arranging food shipments to your town, do you want them to lose service?

The recent rural call completion problem also reminds us that rural communities may bear the brunt of unexpected complications tied to the IP transition, with potentially devastating consequences. As carriers switch to IP technology, it becomes possible for them to route calls through Least Cost Router systems, creating latency and sometimes trapping calls in perpetual loops so calls to or from rural areas do not go through. The Commission has rightly recognized that this issue speaks to our foundational expectation that the phone network will be reliable for all Americans, including those in rural areas, and has opened a proceeding to learn more about exactly why the rural call completion problem is getting worse.[22] But even so, the FCC has received some shockingly inadequate carrier responses to rural call completion complaints. For example, one carrier told the FCC: "We have contacted the [rural complainant] and have successfully resolved this matter by advising [her] that due to living in a rural area she will experience service issues."[23] As discussed below, the DC Circuit's recent decision overturning parts of the FCC's net neutrality rules call into question how the FCC could effectively solve this problem absent classification under Title II.

This is why we need rules of the road: problems will inevitably arise as old systems fade away and new ones arise, but carriers have clearly shown that we cannot simply assume that companies will voluntarily defend the fundamental principles that have made our communications networks great. Meanwhile, 25 states have eliminated or reduced state commission authority over telecommunications services, and 12 states (all of which are in AT&T's incumbent local exchange carrier territory) have eliminated or reduced carrier of last resort obligations.[24] Particularly where the states have effectively written themselves out of the conversation through deregulation, everyday Americans are relying on Federal authorities as their sole defender to protect the reliable, affordable communications access they count on.

The IP Transition and the Elderly

Perhaps the community that stands to be the most impacted by the IP transition is the elderly community. Older Americans have traditionally been later adopters of broadband and wireless technologies. Older Americans also opt for wireline voice services to a greater extent than other demographics, with 89.5 percent of households aged 65 and above living in homes with wireline voice service according to a National Health Interview Survey. In households in the 45 to 64 range, 74.2 percent choose to maintain wireline voice service. Studies show that while more wireless options have increased, this community to prefers to have *both* options available.

Maintaining a network that can support Life Alert technologies for health related emergencies, public safety alerts, and reliable access to 911 capability is critically important for this fast growing demographic. Additionally, although the phone provided by a cable company may generally look and function like a telephone, an older person might not realize the technology used to deliver their voice service is different and not held to the same regulatory protections that they may be dependent on.

While carriers may cite regulation as a reason for the lack of broadband deployment to rural and high cost areas, it has more to do with the low population density

[22]*Rural Call Completion,* Report and Order and Further Notice of Proposed Rulemaking, WC Docket No. 13–39 (rel. Nov. 8, 2013).

[23]FCC Enforcement Advisory, Rural Call Completion: Long Distance Providers Must Take Consumer Complaints About Rural Call Completion Problems Seriously (July 19, 2013), *http://transition.fcc.gov/Daily_Releases/Daily_Business/2013/db0719/DA-13-1605A1.pdf.*

[24]Sherry Lichtenberg, Ph.D., Telecommunications Deregulation: Updating the Scorecard for 2013 National Regulatory Research Institute, at 1, 20–22 (May 2013).

that fails to deliver a sufficient return on investment. The lack of investment in broadband and wireless infrastructure in low population density areas raises serious concerns for the future quality of services available to the elderly community over an IP-based network. The relief from "regulatory burdens" described by AT&T its FCC proposal could have serious consequences for communities that depend on the reliability ensured by wireline regulation like 911 functionality, equal access requirements, and COLR obligations.

Finally, many older Americans also lived on a fixed income, and could be subjected to paying for expensive bundles on upgraded networks in part due to the lack of maintenance or availability of traditional copper based networks. These bundles may not qualify for crucial Lifeline subsidies that provide older and low-income Americans with critical access to phone service.

Moving Forward in the IP Transition

We are now in the midst of the network transition, and the FCC has taken action to gather information and begin creating a framework in which to address the policy questions raised by these technological changes. As policymakers continue working on this issue, the near-term focus should be on collecting data about new technologies, clarifying what standards carriers must meet to replace existing networks with new technologies, and protecting network users throughout and after the transition.

Clarifying the § 214(a) Standard

Before a carrier can discontinue, reduce, or impair service to a community, it must receive authorization from the FCC certifying that the change will not adversely affect the present or future public interest.[25] This system was not designed with the IP transition in mind, and it is simply not suited to situations where a carrier wishes to replace its existing service, still high in demand, with another service. The FCC must therefore take steps now make clear what specific changes would "impair" service under § 214(a) in the context of the network transition, ensuring that its analysis continues to serve the values identified in the unanimous Commission Order beginning the trials process.

There are three areas in particular that need guidance. First, what policies should the Commission adopt as applicable to any new service? These questions would be best handled in the FCC's existing open proceedings addressing these issues.[26] Second, what technical standards for covered services must the new service meet? For example, what consistent voice quality standards should new services meet (as measured in quantifiable—not merely qualitative—measurements)? This should be a pure question of engineering, supported by technical trials and other relevant engineering data, industry standards and best practices, and other technical sources.

Finally, what services must be covered? This is a mixed question of policy and engineering. For example, the FCC has long required providers to permit any network attachment that does not harm the network.[27] Whether the loss of this capability would constitute an impairment or reduction in service is a question of policy. But if the FCC determines that the new service must permit network attachments, then the question of how to do so becomes an engineering question.

More specifically, the FCC should also give guidance for when natural disasters damage networks and carriers wish to replace the network with new technologies instead of rebuilding the copper network. Communities and their residents have always had to deal with temporary network outages after natural disasters, but now that we are in the midst of the phone network transition, we are seeing instances where carriers want to respond to damaged networks by replacing the existing networks with new, untested services, rather than repairing or rebuilding the infrastructure the community has relied on for decades. Like the rest of the phone network transition, this can be an opportunity for better, newer service for the community, but unfortunately we have already seen how it can also force customers—who are already trying to rebuild their lives after a devastating natural disaster—to accept less reliable, more restricted services than what they had before.

Collecting Data to Inform Policy Decisions

The FCC is currently in the process of arranging and approving a series of technical experiments designed to better understand the impacts of new network technologies on consumers. Policymakers should use these trials to better understand

---

[25] 47 U.S.C. § 214(a).

[26] *See* Letter from Angie Kronenberg and Karen Reidy, COMPTEL, to Marlene H. Dortch, Secretary, FCC (Apr. 2, 2014), available at *http://apps.fcc.gov/ecfs/comment/view?id=6017610666*.

[27] *See* 47 C.F.R. § 68 *et seq.*

the transition's technical challenges and opportunities and inform policy decisions going forward.

The trials are an opportunity to collect technical data about new network technologies under a variety of parameters.[28] This data can be used to inform policies that ensure we continue to protect the fundamental values of the network. Ideally, the FCC will be able to use the information collected in the trials to create a detailed "checklist" of technical standards that would guide companies seeking permission under §214(a) to replace their existing networks with new technologies.

It is also worth confirming that the trials, while a useful tool for policymakers, cannot become a vehicle for the transition itself. A trial is not a product launch. The trials must be limited, transparent, carefully controlled experiments, with definite start and end points and definite metrics by which to collect data. Any attempt by a carrier to co-opt a trial into a permanent deployment plan should be firmly rejected to protect customers and avoid distracting from the trials process.

Continuing to Protect Consumers

We cannot let customers be left behind while we are in the midst of these policy debates. We have already seen customers across the country report that they have experienced dropped calls and degraded service quality, and that their carriers responded to their requests for help by aggressively upselling them instead of maintaining the network (as they are legally required to do).[29]

This state of affairs, as reported by consumers across the nation, is unacceptable. Congress and the FCC should both look into the industry practices that led to these complaints, and where appropriate the FCC could also begin enforcement proceedings or information requests. Failure to take any action will only undermine the public's confidence in the network that we have relied on for decades and puts network users across the country at risk of losing access to basic communications service.

Authority to Preserve the Network Compact

As we move forward with the network transition, it is imperative that the FCC continues to have authority to implement policies that serve the network's enduring values.

The Court of Appeals for the D.C. Circuit's recent decision overturning the FCC's no-blocking and nondiscrimination Open Internet rules called into question the FCC's ability to continue applying certain fundamental policies to the phone network as it transitions to IP-based technology.[30] Essentially, the DC Circuit ruled that when the FCC has put something in the Title I "information service" box, it cannot then treat that service like the phone system. This can become a serious problem when the service at issue *is* the phone system. Thus far, the FCC has classified Internet access service as an information service, but has not classified interconnected VoIP as either an information service or a telecommunications service.

To the extent that parts of the phone network's post-transition infrastructure fall under Title I, the FCC now has expanded authority to implement consumer protection rules like extending slamming and cramming rules to IP-based services. However, the DC Circuit's decision casts doubt on the FCC's ability to require VoIP providers to complete all phone calls, prohibit VoIP providers from blocking calls, and implement "carrier of last resort" obligations for VoIP service.

In 2012, the FCC's declaratory ruling addressing the problem of rural call completion was grounded in Title II common carrier authority and the duty to serve everyone.[31] But, as the DC Circuit explained in the net neutrality context, this is precisely the type of action the FCC cannot take for non-common carrier services. So, post-transition, absent reclassification, the FCC would be unable to ensure that all calls go through when someone dials a 10-digit phone number. The FCC could—as it can with net neutrality—require companies to disclose if they are blocking calls or otherwise "managing" traffic in a way that degrades rural traffic. But, as too

---

[28] *See A Brief Assessment of Engineering Issues Related to Trial Testing for IP Transition,* CTC Technology & Energy (Jan. 13, 2014), *http://www.publicknowledge.org/files/CTC-PK%20PSTN %20Report.pdf.*

[29] *See* Letter from Jodie Griffin, Senior Staff Attorney, Public Knowledge, *et al.,* to Julie A. Veach, Chief, Wireline Competition Bureau, FCC (May 12, 2014), available at *http://www .publicknowledge.org/assets/uploads/blog/14.05.12_Copper_Letter.pdf.*

[30] *Verizon v. FCC,* Case No. 11–1355 (D.C. Cir. Jan. 14, 2014).

[31] *Develop an Unified Intercarrier Compensation Regime,* CC Docket No. 01–92, *Establishing Just and Reasonable Rates for Local Exchange Carriers,* WC Docket No. 07–135, Declaratory Ruling (rel. Feb. 6, 2012), available at *https://apps.fcc.gov/edocs_public/attachmatch/DA-12-154A1.pdf.*

many in rural America can already tell you, this has not been effective at curbing the problem.

Similarly the FCC's inability to apply common carriage-like rules to IP-based services could mean the FCC will be unable to implement "carrier of last resort" (COLR) rules after the phone network has transitioned to IP.[32] After all, the obligation to serve the public indiscriminately is at the core of common carriage, so without authority under Title II the FCC could be unable to ensure that everyone in the country has at least one option for standalone basic communications service. Particularly as states deregulate their own COLR rules, the FCC's continued role is critical to achieving universal service throughout and after the transition.

To the extent policymakers ever had the luxury of avoiding the question of the FCC's authority over IP-based services, the phone network transition and the recent net neutrality decision in the DC Circuit make clear that the time for putting off this decision has ended. The underlying technology of the network may be changing, but the fundamental values of the network remain the same, and the FCC must continue to have the authority it needs to protect users and honor the network compact.

Conclusion

The transition of the phone network presents new opportunities and new challenges for policymakers seeking to ensure new networks constitute a true step forward, not a step backward, for everyday Americans. The stakes are high. The choices policymakers make now will impact how the public conducts business, communicates with loved ones, and reaches emergency services. Public Knowledge urges policymakers to follow the basic values that have informed our communications networks since the founding of our country to ensure we can all continue to enjoy a communications network we can count on.

Senator PRYOR. Thank you.
Ms. Honorable?

STATEMENT OF COLETTE D. HONORABLE, PRESIDENT, NATIONAL ASSOCIATION OF REGULATORY UTILITY COMMISSIONERS (NARUC)

Ms. HONORABLE. Good morning, Chairman Pryor, Ranking Member Wicker, and the members of the Subcommittee. Thank you for the opportunity to testify today on the IP transition and its impact on public safety and network resiliency.

My name is Colette Honorable. I have the honor of serving as Chairman of the Arkansas Public Service Commission, and I am especially honored to appear here before my senior Senator, whom I think is an outstanding public servant. I am also testifying in my role as President of the National Association of Regulatory Utility Commissioners.

I applaud the Subcommittee for holding this hearing, which is focused on the proper question, which is which public policy value should be preserved? What consumers care about is that their telecommunications work and are reliable, regardless of the technology used to provide them.

As we transition from traditional circuit-switched technologies to an IP- and wireless-based system, Federal and State policymakers must work together to ensure that emergency 911 service and network resilience do not suffer. Public safety is, indeed, a core value that should not and cannot be compromised.

---

[32] Incidentally, carriers deploying new networks like fiber-based infrastructure may be willing to accept Title II classification when they wish to invoke their common carrier privileges to install fiber over private property or use public rights-of-way. Bruce Kushnick, *It's All Interconnected: Oversight and Action is Required to Protect Verizon New York Telephone Customers and Expand Broadband Services*, Public Utility Law Project of New York, Inc. (May 13, 2014), *http://newnetworks.com/wp-content/uploads/PublicNN3.pdf.*

As Senator Pryor and Ranking Member Wicker know all too well, the recent tornados in Arkansas and Mississippi were another unavoidable reminder of how important these collaborative efforts are to ensure the resilience of our critical infrastructure and the safety of our citizenry. The April EF–4 tornado not only took the lives of many, but damaged hundreds of homes in one county alone.

I am very pleased with the recovery and restoration efforts, which included the immediate response of our Governor, Mike Beebe, the Arkansas Department of Emergency Management, first responders and emergency personnel, and the utility and telecommunication sectors.

Two large cell towers were destroyed, interrupting communications throughout the affected area. However, the carriers responded quickly, bringing in mobile towers that helped to return some level of service. While the situation is devastating, it could have been worse.

Superstorm Sandy demonstrated the frailties of our utility infrastructure, knocking out power for days and weeks, cutting off telecommunications networks. While new IP- and wireless-based systems can be more efficient than traditional landline services, they do not have the same back-up power capabilities as the older networks. Circuit-switched technologies are supported by robust, independent power sources and continue to function during prolonged outages.

Many of the new IP systems rely on a back-up power in the consumer's home. These back-up units are, indeed, the responsibility of the consumer, and therefore, it is important that consumers are educated and are aware about these issues and how they can prolong the life of their infrastructure at home. As more consumers switch to IP-based systems, we must ensure that the technologies provide the same kind of support or that consumers are aware that they may not.

In conclusion, what is important are the values we apply to the communications network, not the technology used to deliver it. FCC Chairman Wheeler espoused the four values of universal accessibility, reliable interconnection, consumer protection, public safety and security. NARUC agrees.

While technology may change, the expectations of consumers do not. Consumers expect the same quality of service, reliability, and access to emergency service to which they have grown accustomed.

When hurricanes, tornados, or other natural disasters unleash their destructive force, they don't discriminate between a copper, fiber, or wireless networks. It is precisely for this reason that we, as policymakers, should not discriminate in applying our values. These values must be applied consistently and in a technology-neutral manner, especially when it relates to public safety.

Thank you for this opportunity, and I look forward to your questions.

[The prepared statement of Ms. Honorable follows:]

PREPARED STATEMENT OF COLETTE D. HONORABLE, PRESIDENT, NATIONAL ASSOCIATION OF REGULATORY UTILITY COMMISSIONERS (NARUC)

Chairman Pryor, Ranking Member Wicker, and Members of the Subcommittee, thank you for the opportunity to testify today on the IP Transition and its impact on Public Safety and network resiliency. Since 2007, I have been a Commissioner with the Arkansas Public Service Commission. Governor Mike Beebe designated me the Commission Chair in 2011. I am also President of the National Association of Regulatory Utility Commissioners (NARUC). NARUC is—like Congress—a *bipartisan* organization. Our members include public utility commissions in all of your States, the District of Columbia and U.S. territories with jurisdiction over telecommunications, electricity, natural gas, water and other utilities. NARUC member commissioners are *the* in-State experts on critical infrastructure in the utility sector and we are very familiar with network resiliency and service restoration issues.

I applaud the Subcommittee for holding this hearing because it is focused on the correct question—which public policy values should be preserved—rather than just on the particular technologies being used to provide services today. NARUC has consistently supported technological innovations that promote more resilient networks and provide better service. But preserving public safety and network reliability, along with other values that customers expect—such as universal access, competition (interconnection), and consumer protection—are also important concerns in *any* technology transition, including this one.

Federal and State policymakers must work together to ensure that emergency 911 services and network resiliency do not suffer as consumers migrate to new technologies. Advances in technology often call for new regulatory policies for both new and existing services.

As FCC Chairman Wheeler noted in a recent posting:

> "When the original 911 rules for wireless providers were first adopted, they were built on the assumption that the primary place consumers would use their wireless phones would be outside. But today, the vast majority of wireless calls are made from indoors, including 911 calls made from wireless phones. Commercial location-based services are raising consumers' expectations—if a smartphone app can locate them within seconds, why can't a 911 call center?" [1]

Why indeed?

To the Chairman's credit, the FCC initiated a proceeding to correct this deficit earlier this year in February. It was an initiative NARUC specifically endorsed by resolution.[2]

Some of these public-interest values present challenges that require the FCC to act—while others require close State-Federal collaborative efforts. The recent tornado in my home State of Arkansas was another unavoidable reminder of how important those collaborative efforts are to ensuring the resiliency of our critical infrastructure and the safety of our citizens.

An EF4 tornado hit Arkansas in April of this year. In one county alone, it destroyed 328 homes; significantly damaged 111 more, and impacted hundreds of others. A new intermediate school which had been rebuilt after a 2011 tornado was once again demolished. It was one of the worst storms during my tenure at the Arkansas Commission and grim evidence that no matter how well utilities and others plan and prepare, the awesome force of nature can and will find vulnerabilities in our critical communications and power infrastructures. It was another reminder of how important it is for policymakers to focus on the right questions.

As we transition to newer technologies, it is crucial for Congress and State and Federal regulators to continue to focus on the right issues and recognize that our collective focus must be the consumer, especially with regard to public safety.

IP-based technologies can be more efficient than the technologies they are replacing. If properly implemented, they also can be more resilient than the old networks in certain ways. Networks that shift to IP-technology are designed to be highly robust to random failures. However, such networks have new vulnerabilities that the earlier technologies did not. For example, so-called "circuit-switch" services are self-powering. The electricity that carries your voice on such system also provides power. IP-based services rely upon external power sources. Therefore if your landline telephone company still provides circuit-switched service, your phone will continue to work even through an electricity outage. If, however, the power goes out in your home and you have an IP-based phone system, you will only retain phone service—even if the rest of the network is operational—as long as your backup batteries

[1] See, Official FCC Blog: "Access and Public Safety: Enduring Elements of the Public Interest," By Tom Wheeler, FCC Chairman, January 30, 20144, available online at: *http://www.fcc.gov/blog/access-and-public-safety-enduring-elements-public-interest*.
[2] See, *e.g.,* NARUC's May 14, 2014 Comments on Wireless E9–1–1 location accuracy requirements, at: *http://www.naruc.org/Filings/14%200512%20NARUC%20Comments%20on%20911%20location%20accuracy.pdf*.

last.[3] During prolonged outages, IP-based residential customers will almost certainly lose phone service. Wireless phones that require external power to recharge once their batteries drain have the same problem.

This is one example where regulatory oversight remains necessary regardless of changes over time in the technology used to provide a service. It is why NARUC has for years consistently urged Congress and Federal regulators to take a technology-neutral approach to regulation.[4] The consumer cares if the phone service works during power outages and emergencies. When she calls 911, she wants that call to go to the right call center—she wants the call center to know where she is. The consumer does not distinguish whether the network provides the service using IP-protocol based or circuit-switched technology. Though sometimes a technology can engender a new problem,[5] the basic reasons why public service commissions and agencies like the FCC were created remain the same.

And there are only two.

First, we regulate where competition[6] is not vigorous enough to adequately protect consumers. Where competition is sufficient to protect consumers and ensure market choice and innovation, then there is a reduced need for regulatory oversight.

Second, we intervene to impose public interest obligations. Regardless of the level of competition, some oversight is always necessary to provide things the market will not. This includes protecting consumers from fraudulent actors and poor service quality, imposing requirements to facilitate or enhanced competitive forces, *e.g.,* (1)

---

[3] See, *e.g.* Giorgianni, Anthony, "Verizon to eliminate free backup batteries for new residential phone customers: Decision by telecom giant could prevent 911 access during blackouts" Consumer Reports (December 12, 2013), online at: *http://www.consumerreports.org/cro/news/2013/12/verizon-to-eliminate-free-backup-batteries-for-new-residential-phone-customers/index .htm.* ("The company said that as of early as December, new FiOS customers who want a backup battery will have to pay a one-time charge of $29.99, buy it elsewhere, or do without. During a blackout, FiOS customers without a battery, household generator, or other type of backup power system will lose their landline voice service, including access to emergency 911.") See also, *U-verse Voice battery backup specifications,* "Upon installation of your AT&T U-verse Voice service, you are provided with a backup battery (or batteries) to help maintain your digital home phone service in the event of a short disruption of electrical power to your home." at: *http://www.att.com/esupport/article.jsp?sid=KB409162&cv=814#fbid=esUgRWuZWBu.*

[4] *NARUC Legislative Task Force Report on Federalism and Telecom* (July 2005). *See also,* NARUC's February 2003, NARUC passed *Resolution Relating To Voice Over The Internet Telecommunications,* available online at: *http://www.naruc.org/Resolutions/voice_over.pdf,* that notes "a significant portion of the Nation's total voice traffic could be transported on IP networks within a few years" and urged the FCC to "confirm its tentative decision that certain phone-to-phone calls over IP networks are *telecommunications services.*" In November 2003, NARUC passed a *Resolution on "Information Services",* at *http://www.naruc.org/Resolutions/info_services.pdf,* cautioning the FCC to consider the negative implications associated with a finding that IP-based services are subject to Title I jurisdiction, including the (i) uncertainty and reduced capital investment while the FCC's authority under Title I is tested; (ii) loss of consumer protections applicable to telecommunications services under Title II; (iii) disruption of traditional balance between Federal and State jurisdictional cost separations; (iv) increased risk to public safety . . . content; (vi) loss of State and local authority over emergency dialing services . . ." Those warnings remain valid today. See also, NARUC's 2008 *Resolution Regarding the Interconnection of New Voice Telecommunications Services Networks,* online at: *http://www.naruc.org/Resolutions/TC%20Interconnection.pdf.* ("NARUC applauds the numerous advances in technology . . . to enable the efficient transmission of voice telecommunications traffic and the continued successes in developing innovative means to deliver voice telecommunications services . . . it is in the public interest for telecommunications carriers to interconnect their networks to exchange traffic in a technologically neutral manner, as provided for under Sections 251 and 252.") *See also,* NARUC's February 2012 *Resolution on Mandatory Reporting of Service Outages by Interconnected Voice over Internet Protocol Service Providers,* asking the FCC to, *inter alia,* extend the mandatory service outage reporting requirements in 47 C.F.R. Part 4 to interconnected VoIP service providers.

[5] Some argue some technology specific rules may be needed to address the reduced resiliency of wireless and fiber networks. But there is no question that competing services should face similar rules. Both rely more on commercial power both at the network level and at the customer premise. The battery backup system installed with FiOS service is the responsibility of the consumer, after one year. There is a similar question, given the increasing number of wireless-only households, of backup power to cell towers. NARUC has raised concerns about the problem and had a panel on the interdependencies between the telecom and energy sectors at our conference last November.

[6] Experts will always argue about how to define a competitive marketplace or what level of competition is needed to eliminate market power concerns but that is a different question and debate. It is also a broader question than the one facing policymakers under the current law. Here the question is, does the 1996 Act allow the FCC to treat functionally equivalent services differently under an ad hoc (FCC-created) regulatory regime. And if it does, how on earth does it make sense for them to do so. Shouldn't competitors be subject to the same set of rules?

requiring local number portability [7] and (2) facilitating interconnection in markets with competing carriers with widely divergent market power, assuring disabled access, emergency calling services and universal service, and, of course, today's topic—assuring a proper level of network reliability, as well as adequate plans that provide robust service restoration after disasters.

With regard to the recent storm in Arkansas, I remain very pleased with the recovery and restoration efforts in Vilonia and Mayflower. This included the immediate response of Governor Mike Beebe and the Arkansas Department of Emergency Management (ADEM), first responders and emergency personnel, along with the prompt response of our telephone companies. As an example of how important connectivity is during an emergency, I received a call at home near midnight after the storm from our Attorney General who was on the ground assisting with rescue efforts in Vilonia. He was concerned about a significant gas leak and requested expedited gas-service disconnection in the neighborhood at issue. I contacted Centerpoint's Regional Vice President and head of Arkansas operations who responded immediately, terminating service to the subdivision where a Level B leak was subsequently discovered. This was but one example of the excellent coordination among all involved in the emergency response effort that night.

As I touched on earlier, the recent storm outages have raised questions about the resilience of these new networks, as both wireless and fiber-based IP services are much more reliant on commercial power from end-to-end.

While regarded by some as old-fashioned, conventional wireline circuit-switched packetized technologies are supported by robust independent back-up power supply resources (*e.g.*, central office standby diesel generators and battery banks), and continue to function during prolonged commercial power outages. As more consumers switch from wireline to IP or wireless service, we must assure that these technologies continue to provide back-up power during outages to maintain emergency communications.

This raises the real question of whether consumers signing up for fiber-based services are fully aware of the trade-offs inherent in shifting to a different protocol. Do they know of the backup power limitations of the network and at their premises? Are they aware of the additional burdens that making this change places upon them to assure their own safety?

For example, Verizon policy states that the battery backup system installed with FiOS service is the responsibility of the consumer, after a one-year warranty.[8] The condition of the battery can dramatically impact the length of backup power a customer will experience in a power outage. While future back-up units may use simple batteries available at the local grocery store or pharmacy, current models require specialized batteries that are not readily available and can be difficult to change. Are most customers who switch aware of and educated about these issues? For many, I suspect the answer is no.

On the wireless side, severe weather can also wreak havoc. As we learned after Superstorm Sandy, there can be problems with backup power at cell towers. NARUC voiced concerns about this by adopting a resolution in July 2013 urging State and Federal regulators "to engage in meaningful dialogue with industry decision makers to develop policies and procedures that ensure telecommunications are maintained during power outages regardless of the technology and the communications protocols used to provide the services." [9]

However, the issue in Arkansas after our recent storm was not a lack of backup power at the cell tower but the complete destruction of some of the towers themselves. There really is no protective measure that can guarantee this type of situation will not occur again. The storm in April destroyed two large cell towers—a 300-ft tower in Vilonia and a 250-ft tower in Mayflower. Multiple wireless providers utilized both towers so coverage to the area was lost across almost all providers. Fortunately, the carriers know this kind of damage is a possibility and, because the equipment shelters were spared, wireless providers brought in temporary mobile tower units the night of the storm and restored some service, as well as additional equipment in the days after the storm.

---

[7] Number portability, which unquestionably facilitates competition, had to be forced on the wireless industry at a time when many considered that sector to be the poster child for a competitive market.

[8] See, *e.g., Verizon battery backup policy,"* available online at: *http://www.verizon.com/Support/Residential/tv/fiostv/general+support/new+to+fios+tv/questionsone/121498.htm#.*

[9] NARUC *Resolution Calling for National and State Collaboration to Ensure Reliable Wireline and Wireless Communications during Power Outages,* adopted July 24, 2013. Available at: *http://www.naruc.org/Resolutions/Resolution%20Calling%20for%20National%20and%20State%20Collaboration%20to%20Ensure%20Reliable%20Wireline%20and%20Wireless%20Communications%20during%20Power%20Outages.pdf*

I commend the carriers for their quick response. While the shorter mobile towers lacked the same coverage and capacity, it was nonetheless a big step forward. Verizon provided mobile towers, Wi-Fi and charging stations at the storm command center within hours of the tornado. AT&T also deployed several mobile charging stations so those in the impacted community could charge their devices and stay connected to friends and loved ones. They waived voice, data and text overage charges for a certain time period as well as set up a hydration station to provide water, snacks and shelter for volunteers. Windstream's service territory was also impacted. The company brought in a temporary trailer to provide power for charging cell phones, etc and it had 10 MB broadband services with computers available to members of the community. They also provided volunteers from other markets to assist in the repair and clean-up effort.

For any policymaker to decide whether any intervention or oversight of a carrier or carriers is necessary, access to information is crucial.

For emergency systems, policymakers at both the Federal and State level need access to outage reporting data submitted by all competing providers, including interconnected VoIP carriers. Without information about the root causes of outages, whether they are on the rise or the wane, we have no way of determining if any action is warranted. Literally, lives hinge on such decisions and, by extension, on access to such data.

In February 2012 the FCC adopted a Report and Order addressing outage reporting requirements by interconnected VoIP providers.[10] NARUC urged the FCC to act on this issue and in a resolution adopted earlier that month called for the agency to: (1) Extend the mandatory service outage reporting requirements in 47 C.F.R. Part 4 to interconnected VoIP service providers; (2) Require interconnected VoIP service providers to report service outage information comparable to that required from other communications service providers, and on a detail level and timeliness that will provide adequate network status information in support of State, county, and local emergency response efforts; (3) Expand the criteria in 47 C.F.R. Part 4 that defines a significant service outage to specifically include VoIP service problems affecting public access to 9–1–1, emergency service communications, utilities, and other telecommunications service providers; and (4) Provide State commissions with the opportunity to have direct and immediate access to the FCC's outage reporting database and to all outage reports filed by interconnected VoIP service providers.[11]

Carriers almost unanimously opposed the FCC's extension of mandatory outage reporting requirements to VoIP technologies. While it is easy to understand why a carrier might not want such data available to policymakers, it is not prudent for those with the responsibility to assure public safety and network resiliency to eschew such information.

Carriers posited a series of unpersuasive "arguments" ranging from outage reporting is a waste of time to the specious argument that the FCC lacks the authority to impose such a mandate on interconnected VoIP providers just because they use IP protocol.[12] Similar arguments proliferate before NARUC member commissions. Carriers have denied some states access to outage data claiming State commissions do not have authority to require reporting solely because of the technology they use to carry their traffic. This is disappointing and contrary to the public interest.

In my state, under our State Emergency Plan, the PSC is responsible for coordinating between the jurisdictional utilities and other State agencies, principally the Arkansas Department of Emergency Management (ADEM). During emergencies, we provide a greater emphasis on the restoration of electric and natural gas service. As a result of State deregulation and existing jurisdictional ambiguity, because of

---

[10] FCC *Report and Order on The Proposed Extension of Part 4 of the Commission's Rules Regarding Outage Reporting To Interconnected Voice Over Internet Protocol Service Providers and Broadband Internet Service Providers;* PS Docket No. 11–82, Adopted: February 15, 2012 Released: February 21, 2012. Available at: *http://www.google.com/url?sa=t&rct=j&q=&esrc=s&source=web&cd=1&ved=0CC0QFjAA&url=http%3A%2F%2Ftransition.fcc.gov%2FDaily Releases%2FDaily Business%2F2012%2Fdb0221%2FFCC-12-22A1.pdf&ei=C02GU8eQOemhsATdm4HYCQ&usg=AFQjCNFk05jz3-notvngKPR21ZABHWcvSA&bvm=bv.67720277,d.cWc&cad=rja.*

[11] NARUC *Resolution on Mandatory Reporting of Service Outages by Interconnected Voice over Internet Protocol Service Providers,* adopted February 8, 2012, available online at: *http://www.naruc.org/Resolutions/Resolution%20on%20VoIP%20Outage%20Reporting.pdf*

[12] FCC *Report and Order on The Proposed Extension of Part 4 of the Commission's Rules Regarding Outage Reporting To Interconnected Voice Over Internet Protocol Service Providers and Broadband Internet Service Providers;* PS Docket No. 11–82, Adopted: February 15, 2012 Released: February 21, 2012. Available at: *http://www.google.com/url?sa=t&rct=j&q=&esrc=s&source=web&cd=1&ved=0CC0QFjAA&url=http%3A%2F%2Ftransition.fcc.gov%2FDaily Releases%2FDaily Business%2F2012%2Fdb0221%2FFCC-12-22A1.pdf&ei=C02GU8eQOemhsATdm4HYCQ&usg=AFQjCNFk05jz3-notvngKPR21ZABHWcvSA&bvm=bv.67720277,d.cWc&cad=rja.*

the FCC's refusal to provide any regulatory classification of VoIP services, we play less of a role in telecom restoration.

It is imperative that we assist in the coordination between the electric and telecommunications utilities in the event of an emergency to understand the timeframes for the restoration of electric facilities and communications facilities, and aid in rescue and recovery efforts. We also assist by providing reports to ADEM on the status of any outages and restoration of electric, natural gas, and to a lesser extent telecommunications service.

We were pleased when the FCC extended its outage reporting requirements to interconnected VoIP providers as NARUC recommended.[13] However, it failed to address our request to provide State commissions with direct and immediate access to the FCC's outage database and to all outage reports filed by interconnected VoIP providers.[14] This is a problem. states play a key role in coordination of outage restoration. We are the "boots on the ground" when disasters strike. Limited access to this information is counterproductive to our joint goal of quick and timely service restoration.

There is concern about the confidential treatment of such data in a handful of states due to their open record laws. However, that should not prevent the sharing of vital public safety information. The FCC should grant immediate access to the outage database and reports for those states meeting the confidentiality requirements. For those that do not meet such requirements the confidentiality issues can be easily resolved by requiring them to issue a certification that the information will be kept confidential, as has been done in the past. In addition, many states have statutory authority to protect highly sensitive or competitive information from public disclosure.[15]

Emergency 911 services are a top priority in every State. Even in states that have adopted deregulatory telecom policies in recent years, all of them have focused on the need for continued oversight of 911 services. Emergency services and network reliability are a core value that does not change with the evolution of technology.

The IP transition is not about regulation or deregulation. The FCC has ample tools in the 1996 Act to eliminate unneeded regulation through the forbearance process.[16] Nor should the debate be technology-focused.

A change in the technology to provide a "functionally equivalent" voice service cannot allow carriers to escape State and Federal disaster recovery, service quality, law enforcement access, universal service, disabled access and interconnection obligations. If the FCC is truly interested in a resilient network and reliable emergency 911 the best thing it can do is provide legal certainty over the classification of VoIP services and apply its policies in a technology-neutral manner.

In conclusion, what is important are the values we apply to the communications network not the technology used to deliver it. Chairman Wheeler has espoused four key values, which he refers to as the "Network Compact". They are universal accessibility, reliable interconnection, consumer protection, and public safety and security. The FCC reiterated these values and noted the need for the agency to work with State, local and tribal governments to uphold these values in its IP-transition

---

[13] February 8, 2012 Letter from James Bradford Ramsay, to FCC Chairman Genachowski and Commissioners McDowell and Clyburn, filed *In the Matter of the Proposed Extension of Part 4 of the Commission's Rules Regarding Outage Reporting to Interconnected Voice Over Internet Protocol Service Providers and Broadband Internet Service Providers,* PS Docket No. 11–82, at: *http://apps.fcc.gov/ecfs/document/view?id=7021858903.*

[14] See *In the Matter of the Proposed Extension of Part 4 of the Commission's Rules Regarding Outage Reporting To Interconnected Voice Over Internet Protocol Service Providers and Broadband Internet Service Providers,* PS Docket No. 11–82, Report and Order, FCC 12–22 (rel. Feb. 21, 2012, at note 230, mimeo at 43: ("We note that, in its ex parte filing on February 8, 2012, NARUC requests that the Commission provide State commissions with an opportunity to have direct and immediate access to outage reporting data and to all outage reports filed by interconnected VoIP service providers. See, NARUC February 8, 2012 Ex Parte Filing. NARUC's request is beyond the scope of this proceeding.")

[15] The Arkansas Commission's authority to keep information confidential is in Ark. Code Ann. Section 23–2–316(b): "(b) (1) Whenever the commission determines it to be necessary in the interest of the public or, as to proprietary facts or trade secrets, in the interest of the utility to withhold such facts and information from the public, the commission shall do so. (2) The commission may take such action in the nature of, but not limited to, issuing protective orders, temporarily or permanently sealing records, or making other appropriate orders to prevent or otherwise limit public disclosure of facts and information."

[16] See, *e.g.,* 47 U.S.C. § 160(c) ("Any telecommunications carrier, or class of telecommunications carriers, may submit a petition to the Commission requesting that the Commission exercise the authority granted under this section with respect to that carrier or those carriers, or any service offered by that carrier or carriers."). See also, 47 U.S.C. § 253.

trials order.[17] NARUC agrees that is what the Act requires. We have adopted our own set of guiding core principles.

In November 2012, NARUC chartered a task force on Federalism to review NARUC's 2005 policies and paper and to determine any changes to those policies required by the changing communications landscape. The resulting whitepaper was unanimously adopted at the NARUC Annual Meeting in November 2013.[18] At its foundation are core principles in line with that of the 1996 Act, and Chairman Wheeler's "network compact." They are: consumer protection; network reliability and public safety; competition; interconnection; universal service; and regulatory diversity.

While technologies change the expectations of consumer do not. Consumers expect the same quality of service, reliability, access to emergency service and the protections to which they have grown accustomed.

When hurricanes, tornadoes or other natural disasters unleash their destructive force they do not discriminate between a copper, fiber, or wireless networks. It is precisely for this reason that we as policymakers should not discriminate in applying our values. These values must be applied consistently and in a technology-neutral manner, especially when it relates to public safety.

Consumers moving to these new services must be educated on their limitations and vulnerabilities as much as they are about the exciting bells and whistles. They must be informed of their new obligations, such as the responsibility to maintain battery backup systems. Failure to provide such vital information could prove deadly. NARUC members deal with network resiliency on a regular basis across the utility spectrum. We stand willing and able to work with this subcommittee, the whole of Congress, the FCC and industry to make sure all Americans enjoy the benefits of a resilient communications network. Thank you for your time and I look forward to any questions you may have.

Senator PRYOR. Thank you.
Ms. Smith?

STATEMENT OF GIGI SMITH, PRESIDENT, ASSOCIATION OF PUBLIC-SAFETY COMMUNICATIONS OFFICIALS (APCO) INTERNATIONAL

Ms. SMITH. Good morning, Chairman Pryor, Ranking Member Wicker, and members of the Subcommittee. My name is Gigi Smith, and I am the President of the Association of Public Safety Communications Officials, or APCO. Thank you for inviting me back to testify on yet another important public safety matter.

APCO is the world's oldest and largest organization of public safety communications professionals. Our members field 911 calls, dispatch critical information to first responders, and manage the communications networks used by first responders.

I have been active in public safety for over 28 years, starting as a 911 call-taker and now serving as the police operations manager for the Salt Lake Valley Emergency Communications Center in West Valley City, Utah. I bring the perspective of an association that is focused on how technology shifts, including the IP transition, impact public safety.

[17] "State, local and Tribal governments and leaders share this challenge, along with other Federal entities. We will work alongside each other to ensure that, as networks transition, public safety is assured, access is universal, competition is promoted, consumers are protected, and the Nation remains well-served by its critical communications infrastructure." From paragraph 9, Page 5, FCC Order, Report and Order and Further Notice of Proposed Rulemaking, Report and Order, Order and Further Notice of Proposed Rulemaking, Proposal for Ongoing Data Initiative, GN Docket No. 13–5, GN Docket No. 12–353, WC Docket No. 10–90, CG Docket No. 10–51, CG Docket No. 03–123, WC Docket No. 13–97, adopted January 30, 2014, available online at: *http://transition.fcc.gov/Daily Releases/Daily Business/2014/db0131/FCC-14-5A1.pdf.*

[18] NARUC Federalism Task Force Report: Cooperative Federalism and Telecom In the 21st Century, adopted November 2013 and available at: *http://www.naruc.org/Publications/Federalism-task-force-report-November-20131.pdf.*

The IP transition will bring a number of benefits. We are fully embracing efforts to bring IP technologies into public safety communications by supporting the FirstNet network, driving Next Generation 911 deployment, and ensuring development of the most effective apps for public safety, among other initiatives.

I would like to now briefly mention a few considerations regarding the impact of the IP transition on public safety.

First, IP-based networks must be reliable, supporting access to 911 communications between dispatchers and first responders, and communications of emergency operations centers and first responder agencies.

Second, IP networks present new vulnerabilities. Service providers should incorporate security procedures, failover plans, and mitigation strategies to best protect public safety communications.

Third, copper networks are self-powered, whereas IP networks rely on power from the consumer electric grid. IP network designs need to consider stand-by power, battery back-up, and other contingency plans.

Fourth, IP networks must maintain the quality of location information for 911 calls, and we encourage exploration of how IP can offer improved capabilities.

Fifth, IP and Next Generation 911 transitions in the public safety community will be more gradual than for nonpublic safety networks. Certainly, additional funding at the national level would support more rapid adoption of next-generation technology by PSAPs and, thus, help public safety keep pace with the industry's IP transition.

Finally, some service providers offer or may require wireless replacements to landlines. We need to preserve existing levels of 911 service in these cases.

In summary, we believe that the IP transition holds great promise. APCO looks forward to working with the Subcommittee and all stakeholders to help guide the best path forward.

Thank you, and I look forward to answering any questions.

[The prepared statement of Ms. Smith Follows:]

PREPARED STATEMENT OF GIGI SMITH, PRESIDENT, ASSOCIATION OF PUBLIC-SAFETY COMMUNICATIONS OFFICIALS (APCO) INTERNATIONAL

Good morning Chairman Pryor, Ranking Member Wicker, and Members of the Subcommittee.

My name is Gigi Smith, and I am the President of the Association of Public-Safety Communications Officials International, or APCO International. Thank you for inviting me back to testify on yet another important public safety matter.

I'm pleased to have the opportunity to highlight the public safety implications of the transition of the Nation's communications infrastructure to IP-based technologies.

I have been active in public safety communications for over 28 years. I started as a 9–1–1 call taker, and then worked my way through the ranks of dispatcher, trainer, supervisor, and I now serve as the Police Operations Manager for the Salt Lake Valley Emergency Communications Center in West Valley City, Utah. My Public Safety Answering Point (PSAP) is a 9–1–1 police, fire, and emergency medical services dispatch center.

Thus, I am very familiar with the impact of changing technologies on the 9–1–1 system and emergency dispatch operations, including how best to ensure that as we embrace new technologies, we preserve, and improve, the safety of the public and first responders.

APCO International is the world's oldest and largest organization of public safety communications professionals, at over 20,000 members. Our members are mainly state and local government employees who manage and operate communications systems for law enforcement, fire, EMS and other public safety agencies. Effectively, our members field 9–1–1 calls, dispatch critical information to first responders, and are integral to the implementation of the critical communications networks used in the field by first responders. In all of these respects, APCO International provides the training, certification, technical, and standards development resources to make the most effective and efficient use of communications technologies in use today or planned for the future.

So as President of APCO, I also bring the perspective of an association that is focused on current and future implications of technological shifts, including the IP transition.

We recognize that the transition of the Nation's communications networks to IP technology will bring many benefits to the public at large, such as the ability to deliver and share content rich video and multimedia messages, with increasing quality.

At the same time, maintaining and improving voice quality remains very important. This is because sometimes the ability of 9–1–1 call takers to hear and pass along subtle background sounds, like someone racking a shotgun, can make a significant difference to the first responder.

Just as another example, IP and related technologies also present us with an opportunity to acquire and utilize data on a large scale, which can help to identify ways to improve efficiencies in emergency response like never possible before.

Indeed, we are fully embracing efforts to bring IP and other advanced technologies into the public safety communications arena. We are actively supporting the FirstNet network, leading the way to responsibly drive implementation of Next Generation 9–1–1 ("NG9–1–1") networks, and ensuring development of the most effective mobile apps for public safety and emergency response purposes, among other initiatives. And there are other public safety communications capabilities that APCO is involved with that also will be impacted by the IP transition, including priority services, emergency alerting, and other existing and growing sources of information such as alarms, sensors, video, and social media.

For the remainder of my testimony, I will offer a few considerations we believe should be kept in mind as we explore how best to preserve the needs of the public safety community.

Reliability

Let me begin with reliability, as this was a term wisely included in the title of today's hearing.

Reliability has a unique importance in public safety—for example, when else would you want to have a more reliable communications capability than during a large-scale emergency? This means that communications networks need to continue to serve the 9–1–1 system, and the first responder community, in the wake of wide-scale physical damage, at times without advance warning, and with rapid and sustained surges in traffic demand.

Over decades, current time-division multiplexing (TDM) copper networks have been built to a very high reliability level of 99.999 percent. While more capable, and feature rich, IP-based networks may be less reliable. Thus, the design of IP-based networks should incorporate a reliable, redundant standard that anticipates real world conditions such as the ability to handle scalable traffic in emergencies. This includes supporting the ability of the general public to reach 9–1–1, the communications between dispatchers and first responders, and the communications systems supporting emergency operations centers and first responder agencies. IP-based networks, when properly designed and implemented, should be both logically and physically redundant.

APCO has been at the forefront of identifying reliable and redundant standards for advanced communications networks. Most recently, APCO worked with the National Public Safety Telecommunications Council to develop and deliver to FirstNet a report on "public safety grade" requirements. While these requirements were designed to provide guidance to FirstNet, many aspects of this report are equally applicable to, and should be part of, any IP network design intended for use or interconnection with public safety.

A related matter is service quality. In the IP world, as in wireless, "quality of service" is a key indicator. Thus, IP networks not only need to be reliable, but deliver the priority and quality of service required for public safety-related communications.

Also related to reliability is recovery and restoration particularly in the wake of severe natural or man-made disasters. On the plus side, IP networks are redundant by design. But as Hurricane Sandy and other disasters have shown, Mother Nature can defeat even the best designed networks. And the rollout of IP networks will involve multiple components serviced by multiple companies, which will require a new level of coordination and associated procedures to ensure rapid service restoration. Further, response plans should include appropriate priority for public safety communications.

Security

As public safety and the industry have already experienced, security is a critical issue. IP networks present new cyber-security and related vulnerabilities as compared to the "closed loop" legacy communications infrastructure. IP networks have been compromised by hackers, and denial of service, spamming, swatting, and other attacks are even more easily perpetrated on an IP-based system, including 9–1–1 networks. Security also becomes a cascading and increasingly complex problem to address, since an all-IP environment introduces a new variety of transport providers, network service providers, and interconnect players.

Thus, service providers should incorporate security procedures, failover plans, and mitigation strategies into their network design to best protect PSAP and other public safety communications.

Power

Copper-based networks are self-powered, whereas IP-based networks rely on power from the consumer electric grid. Thus, IP-based networks are more susceptible to power outages. During power outages, telephone service will not be available unless sufficient backup power is available. Further, IP networks bring a paradigm shift for the consumer, as the customer now becomes responsible for maintaining and ensuring battery back-up. Consider how important it has become for people to be able to-recharge their mobile devices in the wake of power outages that accompany emergencies. In this respect, consumer education will also be key. IP-based network designs need to consider stand-by power, battery back-up, and other contingency plans for power supply.

Location Information

Today's wireline networks typically provide very dependable and actionable, or as we say, "dispatchable" addresses, such as the specific street address of a 9–1–1 caller. Of course, this issue is near to me, as I spoke on the topic of wireless location accuracy in January before this very subcommittee. As I said back in January, the prompt and effective dispatch of appropriate emergency services to any reported event is dependent upon obtaining the best location information possible from the caller. Further, this essential element of dispatching must occur regardless of the technology used to access 9–1–1.

As it relates to the IP transition, ensuring that the general public can reach emergency services in the first place is paramount. At the same time, new technology permits innovative solutions that can improve upon existing location technologies. Thus, we encourage active exploration of how to harness and implement such capabilities from the start.

Impact on 9–1–1 and Next Generation 9–1–1 Networks

We expect that the transition of the Nation's communications networks will be an evolution, following a relatively steady process. But as compared to the transition to NG9–1–1, it will likely occur much more rapidly. To date, IP and NG9–1–1 transitions in the public safety community have been partial, and typically on a PSAP-by-PSAP and carrier-by-carrier basis.

Thus, IP networks will need to interconnect effectively with both legacy 9–1–1 and Enhanced 9–1–1 networks, as well as new text-to-911 services and future NG9–1–1 networks. Further, service providers will have to account for the fact that public safety networks will be provided by a variety of service providers, both private and public. In addition, IP networks will need to adhere to the two prevailing standards that are being deployed for NG 9–1–1 services. One is known as "i3" that some PSAPs are deploying today, and the other is IMS (IP Multimedia Subsystem), which we expect will be the standard used by many PSAPs as well as by FirstNet.

In the current economic environment, local governments are more likely to devote scarce resources first to public safety operations that directly impact both responders and the public (*e.g.,* radios, squad cars, fire engines, ambulances, and related equipment and supplies). As a result, legacy PSAPs are likely to remain operational for some time, and there will be a need to interconnect new IP-based networks to multiple PSAP types for many years to come. Certainly, additional funding mechanisms at the national level would support more rapid adoption of next generation technology at the Nation's PSAPs, and thus help public safety keep pace with the industry's IP transition.

At the same time, public safety's transition to NG9–1–1 will present a number of opportunities and synergies with the evolution of communications networks to IP. Commonalities will include increased multimedia features, new network redundancy options, standardized interfaces for improved interoperability and information sharing, and a broader vendor and service provider ecosystem. APCO has been working with the industry with all of this in mind, and intends to continue to pursue ways to collaborate on network design and implementation to anticipate and meet the needs of the public safety community.

Wireless Options

Finally, let me briefly touch on how the IP transition can lead to wireless replacements of copper and TDM-based networks. In some early offerings, service providers offer wireless replacements as an option to consumers, and in others, a wireless replacement product may be the only option.

In such cases, we believe that certain steps will be necessary to preserve existing levels of 9–1–1 service. We support development of technology that can provide the equivalent of the home address, and detect when the device has been relocated to ensure the address is updated. Also, we recommend that the wireless network serving a wireless-only residence is made as redundant and resilient as possible to withstand natural or man-made disasters and afford sufficient network access and capacity.

In sum, we believe that the IP transition holds great promise for public safety communications, provided that the aforementioned issues are addressed. In this regard, APCO looks forward to working with this Subcommittee, and all stakeholders, to help guide the best path forward.

Thank you for the opportunity to address you, and I look forward to answering any questions you may have.

Senator PRYOR. Thank you.

Ms. Honorable, let me start with you, if I may, and that is kind of pick up where Ms. Smith left off there about 911 service.

As we move forward, does it make sense that 911 service is more of a Federal function or a State function? Specifically, you know, I think we all recognize how important 911 service is, what a great success it has been, but as we transition to IP-based—you know, how should we make sure that our 911 service has the integrity that it has up to this point?

Ms. HONORABLE. Thank you, Senator, for the question.

The NARUC community believes that it is a proper State function. I believe the success that we have enjoyed thus far has been precisely because of the ability of the states to work very nimbly and with flexibility within their borders to not only coordinate and have oversight, but also to respond in emergent situations.

When I think back over the severe weather events that we have had over the past few years—and we have, indeed, had many, as many of the members of the Subcommittee have—the ability of first responders of our State Department of Emergency Management, of our Governor's office, of the local and county officials, as well as the State public utility commissioners, to participate very aggressively with coordination efforts, even at heightened levels than ever before, it is imperative that we have the ability to respond quickly, that we have the ability to oversee 911 efforts locally because the ultimate goal is safety.

The ultimate goal is public safety and ensuring that we use every tool to respond as promptly as possible, and the best way to do so is to ensure that that is occurring at the State level.

Senator PRYOR. Are there any States, though, that have State laws that would prohibit the State PSE or PUC, whatever they call it in their State, to do 911 requirements on an IP system? Are you aware of any?

Ms. HONORABLE. No, I am not aware. There are certainly other State prohibitions with regard to telecommunication services more broadly. As you know, many states have undergone deregulation. But certainly, the 911 core functions are carried out at the State and local levels.

Senator PRYOR. Mr. Banks, let me ask you, I have a concern about us going to IP, and some of you all have mentioned this. I mean, obviously, there is great innovation with it, and there is a lot of good things with it. I don't want to say it is all bad because it is not at all.

But we all know and our experience has been that when a lot of people are on the Internet, sometimes it runs slower, and we talked about the power, the need for, you know, electricity, and if electricity goes out, you lose your power. So how do we resolve that with—how do we resolve that in the 911 world, or when there are emergencies or some crisis, that too many people get on the system, and how do we make sure as we go forward that we don't have that problem?

Mr. BANKS. Thank you.

There is always an issue around disasters when networks can be overloaded, and that can be a wireless network, a traditional copper network, or another network. I think the first thing that puts us in a better position for all this than we were a decade or two ago is that there are multiple networks throughout the country.

So, in general, people can use their traditional wireline network. Their neighbor might be on a cable network. There are four or more wireless networks, and 90-plus percent of Americans have at least one mobile phone in the home. So there are these multiple networks people can turn to, and if any one network gets overloaded, that doesn't mean no one can get through to 911.

But fundamentally, you are asking a very good question about designing robustness into these systems, and that—that is a challenge for our industry, the wireless cable industries, and the public safety community to work together to make sure that there are the right number of trunks to PSAPs, that there are back-ups and overflow systems.

So, you know, this is one of these technological challenges we are working through with this transition and working through at DHS, with APCO and the public safety commission, with the FCC, and you know, we are very focused on that.

Senator PRYOR. Senator Wicker?

Senator WICKER. Thank you.

Let me ask about the transition between the copper line networks and IP, fiber. It obviously doesn't all happen at once. So there is a lag there.

Let me start with Mr. Banks. Substantial geographic areas—and therefore, substantial numbers of individuals—will be living in areas that will continue to be served by copper, which we call TDM, and others will be in the transition to IP areas. How will providers and your members ensure that these communities will maintain the ability to communicate with areas served by all IP networks?

Mr. BANKS. Well, thank you.

I think that the customers you are talking about, the TDM or the old-fashioned copper customers, are all customers of the members of USTelecom. They are our customers. We have been serving them for decades. Our companies have every intention of making sure those people can call whomever they want, and when people call them, that those calls go through.

So I think the commitment is there. I think there are occasional unfortunate rural call completion issues that your question probably touches on. But our members who serve these people every day are going to make sure that those calls can go through, for the next—for however long it takes to get through the IP transition.

Senator WICKER. Do you need any help from—from the Congress in that regard?

Mr. BANKS. There is a substantial effort at the FCC to understand some of these rural call completion issues going on, and the FCC is gathering data from across the industry. So I think—we are very involved in that, in the provision of data, and I think we need to see the outcome of that FCC investigation.

Senator WICKER. Let me toss this topic to you, Mr. Schulzrinne. Are there any novel technical challenges to maintaining connectivity in this incremental area-by-area phaseout?

Mr. SCHULZRINNE. Yes, I believe there are. The challenge is always when you have an old technology and a new technology. The danger is that investment in the old technology lags and that there are complexities that are incurred because you need to interconnect the old technology to the new technology.

I briefly mentioned the CAMA trunk problem, where even in areas which are now served by IP, for example, most of the cable customers are typically on Voice over IP systems, they still reach PSAPs through these legacy trunks, which are often capacity limited, that are brittle, poorly maintained in terms of their vendor support, and very few people still understand how they operate. So the transition, I believe, in many cases, if it happens faster across the network, can prevent these types of interruptions.

For the call completion issues, I do believe there are opportunities that as we transition to Voice over IP-based interconnection, as opposed to TDM-based interconnection, that the number of places where things can go wrong decreases.

Similarly, the Commission has started an effort, as part of its investigation of telephony numbering, to improve the data bases, which, at least in some cases, are implicated in making it difficult to route calls to the correct destinations and leads to call failures.

Senator WICKER. Ms. Honorable, do our friends at the State regulatory level have any insights to offer in this regard?

Ms. HONORABLE. Yes sir, Senator Wicker. Yes, we do, thank you.

We have been engaged with the FCC, even at the highest levels. I have personally met with Chairman Wheeler about the IP transition issue, and I want to applaud the FCC for engaging the states.

They recognize that we have a significant role to play in aiding in a smooth transition, and we have been particularly interested and concerned about doing our part to ensure a smooth, or smoother, transition. And we hope to watch with great interest the IP trials, and we have been following and working with the FCC and its staff to ensure that State regulators are involved, offering feedback.

Again, the ultimate goal that we share is the same, and it is to ensure public safety, but also from a regulatory perspective, ensuring the same tenets we have come to know, the same quality of service, the same ability for consumers to have optionality, and for them to have consumer protections as well.

Senator WICKER. Thank you all.

Ms. HONORABLE. Thank you.

Senator PRYOR. Senator Klobuchar?

STATEMENT OF HON. AMY KLOBUCHAR,
U.S. SENATOR FROM MINNESOTA

Senator KLOBUCHAR. Well, thank you very much, Senator Pryor, for holding this important hearing.

Senator Wicker, if there is one thing every person is concerned about, I know from my former job as a prosecutor, is public safety, and we need to make sure that these new technologies are functional.

There are many opportunities. You know, firefighters walking into a building that will maybe be able to see immediate blueprints or video of what is in there. And you have Minnesotans who get stranded out on snowmobiles when they break down, and they are—their only hope is to have some kind of a GPS system if they are lost. And we have seen some really good rescues, actually, because of technology, but we know that there are also challenges.

I am the Chair of the Next Generation 911 Caucus, and I continue to be an advocate for deploying this community technology and this modern technology and our efforts. As with many members of this subcommittee, I have been concerned about call completion. It is not going to help if people are making 911 calls, if they can't complete them. And this is especially, as you know, Ms. Smith and Ms. Honorable, is a problem in the rural areas.

And what I wanted to know from the NARUC perspective, is if you have been supporting the action by the FCC? As you know, they just issued a new consent decree, announced yesterday, with Matrix Telecom, and can you expand on how this issue is of a concern to public safety if we can't complete the calls?

Ms. HONORABLE. Senator, thank you for the question.

Thank you for your concern, also we share in that, on both points that you have mentioned. One, regarding public safety. And after Hurricane Sandy, NARUC issued a strong resolution, which calls for heightened coordination, particularly among the utility and telecommunication sectors.

For some time, we have been operating within our own silos, but the lesson we have learned from Sandy and the derecho storm and others is that there is a strong symbiotic relationship between both the utility sector and telecommunications. They need one another.

The telecom sector can't do an effective job without the electric infrastructure, and the electric infrastructure can't communicate and get the lights back on without a strong telecommunications effort to restore service once there has been an interruption. So we have been very active there.

Particularly also on call completion, too, the second issue that you raised, we have also issued resolutions on call completion. We commend the FCC's efforts, even yesterday, with regard to that consent decree.

This is such an important issue. The calls have to go through because lives are on the line, and we recognize that. And we are very committed to continuing to raise these issues and aiding where we can, as State regulators, to making sure that we see this through because lives depend on it.

Senator KLOBUCHAR. Thank you very much.

And Senator Fischer has been working with me on that effort, and I appreciate your help on this as well.

We are starting to see text to 911 services, as I mentioned, being launched, and someday we may be able to see, as I mentioned, video to 911 services. Ms. Smith, how do you view the potential for these innovations, and how will the IP transition help or hinder these efforts? What is the balancing act that we need to see to ensure that the new networks have what they need to provide the services?

Ms. SMITH. Well, there is a balancing act, and as Mr. Wicker mentioned earlier, this is an exciting transition. So, for me personally, being the police operations manager of a 911 center, it is exciting to see what the future lies ahead, to be able to have these resources for my responders and to be able to offer them the information that is needed.

But with the balancing act, there are pros, and there are concerns. And those concerns or those challenges, as we have mentioned earlier, come with—you know, we need to have reliability, and we have to have security. Reliability. We need to ensure that those systems are up, and in the time of need, our citizens can call in and reach 911 and get the help that they need.

But we also need to be aware of the security issues. There is, you know, cybersecurity to be aware of—TDOS, Telephony Denial of Service, swatting, spamming, those types of things. So that our systems aren't taken down, but instead, we know that they are reliable, that they are there when they are going to be needed.

Senator KLOBUCHAR. And one last question. When we passed the Spectrum Act, I included an amendment that would allow revenue from the incentive auction that wasn't allocated to FirstNet or paying down the deficit to go to Next Generation 911 upgrades, including the implementation of IP-enabled emergency services and applications. We expect the auction to put—take place next year.

I know we hope the auction raises enough revenue to provide these resources to upgrade our 911 systems, but in the meantime, what other Federal resources are available to help PSAPs as they work to keep up with this evolution to IP?

Ms. SMITH. I think funding is a very important question, and I don't have the answer specifically as what other fundings are available, but I can definitely look into that, and we can respond back.

But I do—I would like to say that, you know, funding is important in as much as that, I know my own center, we just went through where we are now able to connect with IP, and I know how much we spent, just under $400,000. And with that, that is just for the equipment only. That doesn't include the training, the personnel, and the other equipment that is going to come with it.

Times that by approximately 6,000 PSAPs that are across the Nation. There is going to be a large cost, and it is very important that—you know, we understand and we are very appreciative that those funding sources may come, and will be coming later, but the same time, we need to have something immediate in order to ensure that public safety does not lag behind and that we can keep up with the industry.

Senator KLOBUCHAR. Thank you.

Senator PRYOR. Thank you.

Senator Johnson?

STATEMENT OF HON. RON JOHNSON, U.S. SENATOR FROM WISCONSIN

Senator JOHNSON. Thank you, Mr. Chairman.

I apologize for not being here for all of the testimony, but Mr. Banks, I am a numbers guy. It looks like your testimony had more numbers——

[Laughter.]

Senator JOHNSON. —so I want to try and define the problem here. We are talking about transition from, you know, copper to IP. How much has already been transitioned? I mean, how much do we have left to go?

Mr. BANKS. Well, I would say that if you look across America's households, about 25 percent still have regular, old-fashioned POTS, copper-type phone service. I would say the vast majority of America's businesses have switched to IP-based systems.

Senator JOHNSON. Of that 25 percent, though, how much—how many have easy access to upgrade, to make the transition?

Mr. BANKS. Uh——

Senator JOHNSON. Or is it all, is that 25 percent just a problem?

Mr. BANKS. No, no. So the most—much of that 25 percent also has a cable system available or, like many households, could switch to wireless. The upgrade path for those homes to go to IP is—depends very much on where they are. In some of the more rural areas, it is a longer term issue.

Senator JOHNSON. That is what I am trying to find here. What percentage of people that haven't transitioned is the real problem? Where we really have to be concerned about, you know, companies like yours, you have made significant investments, $671 billion, into—you know, into the infrastructure, but what percent is really the problem?

Mr. BANKS. That is a difficult number to give you, but having the FCC follow through on the right universal service reform to ensure that people that have these really old—the older networks in rural areas, that there is a business case to upgrade.

Senator JOHNSON. Mr. Schulzrinne, you look like you want to jump in here?

Mr. SCHULZRINNE. I just wanted to comment from a technology perspective and, as Mr. Banks alluded to, somewhat different circumstances. So the one is where only TDM is available, and that is, I think, a relatively small number of places, but they exist where no robust IP networks exist and, in particular, where not all rural telecom providers offer Voice over IP services because that would run over copper.

Senator JOHNSON. So just give me a percent. Are we talking about 1 percent? Are we talking 10 percent?

Mr. SCHULZRINNE. It is hard to pin that down.

Senator JOHNSON. I am just looking for a ballpark.

Mr. SCHULZRINNE. Order of magnitude, I would say, it is probably in the 5 percent-ish range.

Senator JOHNSON. OK.

Mr. SCHULZRINNE. But that changes on a year-by-year basis.

Senator JOHNSON. But again, we are talking about we have got a 5 percent problem here.

Mr. SCHULZRINNE. Yes, the problem is, however, also one where a number of consumers have chosen to retain a landline because they value the features of a landline. So, indeed, one carrier has recently offered a 911-only service on a traditional landline for a relatively modest fee, presumably to address consumers that want to retain those or that do not want to subscribe to, say, a cable service.

Senator JOHNSON. OK, I know there has been some discussion, I think, action, of course, as to how we are going to actually regulate broadband. Anybody here on the table really want to regulate broadband under the telecom rules? Is there anybody?

I mean, guys, I assume nobody wants to do that? Or——

Ms. GRIFFIN. I would say that I think that the values that underlie the phone network apply just as much as we move to the next generation of communication services and broadband. I think that how those rules look may be a little different than what we have done in the phone network because it is a different technology, and it operates differently.

But at the end of the day, we still want everybody to have access to what the basic service is, and as that moves to broadband, then we need to make sure that we still have rules that are ensuring everybody has access to that, too.

Senator JOHNSON. Ms. Griffin, in notes on your testimony, it sounds like you are not necessarily believing the broadband companies have an incentive to make sure that, you know, the majority of the calls go through and that you really think Government has to—is that—is that your position? Do you really need Government to force broadband providers to make sure that their service is excellent?

Ms. GRIFFIN. I think that—we have seen some reports where there have been failures, like cases in rural call completion, and the lesson I take there is that even in situations where there may not be any bad actors, new technologies can create situations where nobody really has an incentive to absolutely guarantee that calls go through, and then maybe——

Senator JOHNSON. Do you think Government can absolutely guarantee that every call goes through? Do you think Government really has got a better capability, as opposed to the broadband carriers themselves, to provide excellent customer service. If you have a company and you are providing a service, if it doesn't work very often, don't you think customers are going to switch to a different company?

Don't you think competition would actually do a far better job than having the heavy hand of Government try and guarantee that, which, I don't think it would do?

Ms. GRIFFIN. Well, I think in too many areas, competition doesn't exist or isn't robust enough to really guarantee that people are going to have a meaningful choice, particularly, say, if they are using a heart monitor, and they may be able to switch to a wireless service, but it wouldn't support the heart monitor or something like that, or if the new service isn't affordable.

So I think that the essential promise of the phone network is that when you make a call, it goes through, and that should be the goal of the Government is to make sure that we are fulfilling that promise.

Senator JOHNSON. Mr.—I am running out of time, but Mr. Banks, would you just like to respond to Ms. Griffin there?

Mr. BANKS. I think that the vast majority of Americans have multiple choices for how they communicate, and that interconnection is part of how the whole industry works. So completing calls is essential to any company being able to sell voice service, and you see this on the wireline side.

On the wireless side, the Government does not get involved, telling wireless companies how to connect and not connect. And interconnection happens in the free market there. There is no reason to think it wouldn't happen throughout the rest of the industry.

Senator JOHNSON. Thank you, and thank you, Mr. Chairman.

Senator PRYOR. Senator Ayotte?

STATEMENT OF HON. KELLY AYOTTE,
U.S. SENATOR FROM NEW HAMPSHIRE

Senator AYOTTE. Thank you, Mr. Chairman. I want to thank all of you for being here.

I want to follow up on some of the points Senator Johnson has made. As I understand it, the purpose of the Universal Service Fund is really to build out capacity—used to be hard lines, now we are looking at broadband because of what we are talking about today in terms of an IP transition, which makes sense, in terms of technology.

I represent a state that gets really shortchanged under this fund, 37 cents on the dollar, and, I would love to have any of you drive around New Hampshire with me in the rural areas, and you can see that we really have significant needs that aren't being addressed. So I have introduced legislation to make it more equitable, reform this fund. I want the FCC to act further, to reform universal service.

But, Mr. Banks, when we are thinking about this percentage that Senator Johnson asked you about, really what we are talking about perhaps are rural areas where you are not going to have the business incentive to build out capacity, and that, as I understand it, is why we have the Universal Service Fund. So what are your thoughts, in terms of IP transition, as a way of more effectively using the Fund, and what opportunities do you see for rural America with the Universal Service Fund in this IP transition?

Mr. BANKS. Yes.

Senator AYOTTE. And please correct me if I am wrong in terms of what I think the purpose of this fund is in terms of what we are trying to accomplish here.

Mr. BANKS. No, you are absolutely right. The purpose of the USF fund is to connect Americans. The FCC is engaged in a major reform of a big part of that fund, the part of the fund for larger companies, and increasing the funding available to larger companies to serve people who wouldn't be served otherwise.

The FCC—that was an FCC 2011 reform order. The FCC is still working to implement that, to operationalize it. Hopefully, that will be in place by 2015, and for the larger companies, funds will flow in a much more targeted way, more funds to connecting people in census blocks where they have no options, no other service.

Senator AYOTTE. What about the smaller companies as well? I mean, as we think about——

Mr. BANKS. Right.

Senator AYOTTE.—this IP transition, how do we think it will impact competition? I think that is an important issue for consumers, and also as we look at reform of the USF fund. And you know, I have heard a lot of concerns, obviously, with this transition from rural carriers as well.

Mr. BANKS. Right. So part two of the USF reform is reforming the smaller company, the rural company fund. The FCC made some reforms that were ill advised. To the FCC's credit, and Chairman Wheeler, he has taken those off the table and is going to issue a notice of rulemaking to modernize the fund for rural carriers, just like they modernized the fund for larger carriers. That is a very big deal and very important to get that right.

In terms of rural carriers and the IP transition, many rural carriers have invested heavily in broadband and fiber and IP. So, in many rural areas, IP services are available. The right reform of the fund should help a lot with that.

Senator AYOTTE. Mr. Schulzrinne, would you like to comment on this? I am sure you have some thoughts on it.

Mr. SCHULZRINNE. Yes, let me comment on the technical aspect. Thank you for the question.

The IP transition, unlike in the old—older days where, essentially, rural meant you had to extend copper lines to remote areas, now offers several choices that will make it, hopefully, possible to cost effectively reach all Americans, whether that is through fiber, the long-term, probably preferred option in terms of capability; extending the capability of copper; fixed wireless; and in really remote areas, satellite.

It is important to provide robust broadband to all Americans. It allows modern applications—voice, as well as video and other applications—to function well. And indeed, to explore these technologies in new ways of providing broadband—robust broadband services as part of a reform effort, Mr. Banks mentioned we are looking at an experiment to provide funding to both traditional and nontraditional providers to extend broadband into rural areas.

We have received over 1,000 indications of interest from a wide variety of organizations—electric utilities, traditional carriers—communities working well with these organizations to explore providing robust, mostly fiber, but also robust wireless services, into areas that are not currently being served.

So I believe that technology transition gives us additional opportunity to do that cost effectively and on a schedule which may be more aggressive than what we have been able to do in the past, where we had to rely on one technology only.

Senator AYOTTE. Well, that actually would be good news for many rural areas because, as you know, having the ability to connect can determine the economic viability of rural areas as well. So I see this as a very important jobs issue.

So, thank you.

Senator PRYOR. Senator Nelson?

STATEMENT OF HON. BILL NELSON,
U.S. SENATOR FROM FLORIDA

Senator NELSON. A hurricane approaches, knocks out the power. Somebody is in dire straits in their home, and they need to make a 911 call. In the copper wire, that power source is there. In fiber optic, there has generally got to be a power source in the house or a battery back-up.

What do we do? Ms. Smith?

Ms. SMITH. Yes, that is very important. Thank you for the question.

There is going to be a paradigm. There is going to be the change. Our consumers, they are used to that. They are used to just picking up the phone, and it works for them.

And I think a lot is going to have to come back on education, and that is going to have to be from the industry and both from the PSAPs ourselves to educate the consumers how important that back-up power is going to be, whether that be, as we, in public safety, call our "plan B," meaning that we have those sources available to us, whether that be supplied with the equipment, whether I know—I know my equipment well. I know if it takes an extra battery and how I am going to recharge that battery.

But, that is so important, again, to bring to their attention so that they know what the expectation is, and they know that they could have those challenges ahead of them, so that they can reach help when they need it.

Senator NELSON. Well, you have got a lot of educating to do, if it is anything like smoke detectors and the batteries in the smoke detectors.

Ms. SMITH. Well, and absolutely, I realize that. Think about how stressed you are now when you have your smartphone, your cell phone, and you see that the battery is getting low, and you have nowhere to plug it in. Imagine in an emergency, you need to make that phone call, you need help, and you don't have the power that is necessary.

So to be able to educate and to put that information out there, but also to ensure that the industry is creating what is necessary, whether it be, you know, those battery packs they are putting into the homes or making those available to the customer so that they can have those in their time of need.

Senator NELSON. Anybody else?

Mr. SCHULZRINNE. Let me comment on that from a technology perspective briefly. The opportunities are that I think industry is learning, and based on consumer experience I believe partially that, I think, could help to make that less onerous than it is for smoke detectors, for example.

First, unlike for smoke detectors, these devices typically are re-chargeable batteries. So, in most cases, they should be charged up. However, often, the duration that they provide may be sufficient to bridge short disruption, but not longer disruption.

I believe, and this is reflected in some of the comments that our technological advisory council has been offering, is that there are opportunities, for example, with user exchangeable batteries. So you can go to the drugstore and pick up new D cells, for example, and some carriers are starting to do that.

With standardized connectors, so that you can use, for example, the backpacks that some people have on their cell phone to power their own connectivity. And importantly, to reduce the power consumption of network units. That has two benefits. It reduces the use of energy during normal times, but it also allows households to sustain operation, and I believe it is important to sustain it for both voice and Internet connectivity for much longer duration than we are currently able to do.

Senator NELSON. Well, that is a good suggestion from a technological standpoint. Say, for example, with an elderly population, the easier that you can make it to recharge those batteries, for example, what you just suggested, with the kind of thing that we do with cell phones, that is—that interconnectability so that a senior citizen knows what to do, that is a good suggestion.

Thank you.

Senator PRYOR. Thank you.

Senator Markey? And I am actually going to turn the gavel over to you, Senator Nelson, because they need me for a quorum in another committee. So, thank you.

Senator Markey?

STATEMENT OF HON. EDWARD MARKEY,
U.S. SENATOR FROM MASSACHUSETTS

Senator MARKEY. Thank you, Mr. Chairman, very, very much.

It was just 18 years ago, when the Congress passed the Telecommunications Act of 1996. I was the House author, and not one home in America had broadband in February of 1996. So, today, a 12-year old believes that broadband and a 50-inch HD screen is a constitutional right, huh?

[Laughter.]

Senator MARKEY. That is how quickly it all moved. No two ways about it. And simultaneously, you know, out of my committee, we moved the spectrum for the third, fourth, fifth, and sixth cell phone license. It was all bottled up, just bottled up, so that a couple of companies, you know, controlled everything, and you couldn't have a Facebook and eBay and Amazon or Hulu, YouTube. You couldn't have all these other issues because they were all bottled up by companies, competitors that did not want to see that kind of a competition.

44

And what we had to do as part of that act was to ensure that reliability, competition, consumer choice, economic growth were all a part of this, and a trillion dollars worth of private sector investment went into the marketplace because of those couple of laws. Trillion dollars of private sector investment, because there was more opportunity for people to get out there with their new ideas, their new products, their new ways of doing business. But they needed the Government to set the rules so the private sector could act.

And the principle definition of the Act was that everything was going to be technology neutral. We weren't going to decide. The marketplace was going to decide. So we need to make sure that the system is reliable. We have to make sure that public safety remains at the core, and we have to make sure that the phone network works every single time. We learned that again at the marathon bombing in Boston. We each learned it in each one of our communities over and over and over again.

Ms. Griffin, what implications on public safety does the D.C. Circuit's Net Neutrality decision have for the transition to IP?

Ms. GRIFFIN. Thank you.

That court decision has tremendous implications for the phone network and the IP transition. One lesson that we can take from it is that if the FCC has put a service into the information service box, in terms of its regulatory classifications, the one thing it can't do is make it act like the phone network, and that becomes a huge problem when the service we are talking about is the phone network.

So if we can't—if the FCC can't require carriers to complete every call and make sure that we have complete reliability in the phone network without reclassifying these services as Title II telecommunication services, then that is what it needs to do to avail itself of the authority it has.

Senator MARKEY. And I agree with you. Ms. Griffin, the chairman is from Florida, but how should we evaluate the results of AT&T's IP trials in Florida and Alabama? What would a success look like?

Ms. GRIFFIN. I think successful trials would be trials that have rigorously and objectively collected data that—on a variety of parameters that is designed to inform us about these new technologies so we know, for example, what is the impact on voice quality, what is the impact on reliability? And trials that do so transparently and continue to protect consumers throughout the trials so that, even though this is an experiment and we are learning, we have safeguards to know that people won't be left behind during the trial.

Senator MARKEY. Thank you.

And there are concerns that the IP transition will impact vulnerable populations—including seniors, minorities—disproportionately, who rely on traditional telephone service. What steps have to be taken to ensure that the broadband services and other services are provided to the public, regardless of age or economic circumstances? Does anyone want to take that so they can give us an answer as to how we should do that?

Ms. HONORABLE. Senator Markey, thank you for the question.

I believe, and certainly, NARUC, the National Association of Regulatory Utility Commissioners has been very engaged with the FCC on this issue, and I believe that a very broad stakeholder involvement process is critical. It is critical to make sure that we leave no consumers on the side of the road, particularly where so many of our states have substantial rural areas, significant senior populations, significant minority populations. It takes an "all hands on deck" approach, and NARUC is certainly part of this process going forward.

Senator MARKEY. And Ms. Griffin, there are—some people say that because we are moving toward mobile, we really don't have to keep a lot of the protections on the books from the 1996 Act for the land-based, you know, wireline services. What are the potential unintended consequences of removing protections that were built into the 1996 Act?

Ms. GRIFFIN. Well, I think, first of all, whether it is a mobile call or a landline call, when someone places a phone call, they expect it to work, and a lot of times, they are expecting the exact same guarantees they had on the traditional copper network, even if they are making the call via a wireless network. Also, wireless networks rely on wireline networks for backbone—for their backbone service. So we can't ignore wireline just because more people have cell phones.

And additionally, 100 million people still have traditional copper-based service, and 85 million of those people have it in addition to another type of voice service, usually wireless. I don't think that is because they like paying two bills. I think that is because they get protections from the landline service they don't get elsewhere.

Senator MARKEY. OK. Do you all agree that we should keep the protections from the 1996 Act on the books, even as we move more toward a wireless world? Do you all agree with that? Ms. Smith?

Ms. SMITH. Yes.

Mr. BANKS. Yes. I think from our perspective, the network——

Senator MARKEY. Ms. Honorable? Mr. Banks?

Mr. BANKS.—compact idea that Chairman Wheeler has articulated is—is something we believe in, and defining those and figuring out how to best apply them to everybody is a challenge.

Senator MARKEY. OK. Thank you all so much.

Thank you, Madam Chair.

Senator KLOBUCHAR [presiding]. Thank you very much.

I have a few more questions, and then I think we are going to be joined by Senator Booker.

Our public alert systems are crucial to making sure that the public is notified of any oncoming danger. In my State, it is very important because of tornados. We actually have a lot of tornado touchdowns in Minnesota.

Mr. Schulzrinne—OK, how do you say it again?

Mr. SCHULZRINNE. Schulzrinne.

Senator KLOBUCHAR. Schulzrinne. OK. It is almost as good as my name——

[Laughter.]

Senator KLOBUCHAR.—so there we go. How will pubic alert systems operate in an IP-enabled world?

Mr. SCHULZRINNE. So public alert systems, currently, we have essentially a hybrid system between a traditional system, namely, the Emergency Alert System, that uses radio and television largely; the wireless system that is limited to very short messages; and a backbone system, if you like, that is behind the scenes, namely, IPAWS, that distributes various messages to both.

I believe that as we move to a mostly IP environment, that the existing components will continue to be fulfilling a very vital role, but that we can supplement those. In particular, the limitations that we have of the wireless emergency alert system, the short messages may no longer be necessary in an all-IP environment, and importantly, we can now leverage new ideas on how to distribute wire—alerts.

For example, since many people no longer watch TV or listen to radio continuously, they have the opportunity, for example, to inject alerts into Internet content, be it video streaming or maybe through advertising networks that might be placing—that people might be viewing.

So we have to see that as an integrated system that is available regardless of technology, maintains the legacy protections and capabilities, because many of those are robust in large-scale disasters in particular, but also provides much more precise targeting and much more detailed information.

Finally, it is important to not just think about the first minute or so of an alert, as important as they are, but also to think about the whole lifecycle of a disaster. For example, during Sandy, it was important to inform consumers as to where could they get gasoline, where could they find grocery stores that were open, what roads were passable. All of those were much more readily conveyed by maps and other IP-based information, and so we need to integrate those longer-term recovery functions with the important short-term, seek shelter, immediate response type of capabilities.

Senator KLOBUCHAR. OK. Thank you.

We have talked here about how we can see failure with IP over fiber, particularly during natural disasters, and that depending on the situation, copper technology can be more effective. Mr. Banks, what can be done to ensure that people are able to communicate effectively via IP technology? Do you think this transition to fiber is the answer?

Mr. BANKS. OK. So I think there are a number of things, like Mr. Schulzrinne has said. There is a lifecycle to this. So disaster preparedness is important, and there are sites like Ready.Gov that our industry contributes to that can help people think through what they need to do first.

Alerting is very important, reliability, and then restoration. So we have talked a lot about copper and the advantage it has in powering, which is a significant and meaningful advantage. But we shouldn't overlook that fiber has some advantages. Fiber is generally a more reliable technology and less prone to going out, and in general, fiber is quicker to restore than copper.

Senator KLOBUCHAR. Mm-hmm.

Mr. BANKS. So when a tree falls over on a power line and a phone line, if the phone line is fiber, it is quicker to restore than for copper. So it is a balancing act here, and I think we recognize that the copper network and the switches that run it are deteriorating. There aren't people making those switches. There aren't—there is not a real market for spare parts. People are retiring——

Senator KLOBUCHAR. Are you aware of the copper theft issue?

Mr. BANKS. There is the copper theft issue. Yes. It is very driven by the market price of copper.

Senator KLOBUCHAR. Mm-hmm.

Mr. BANKS. And so, the movement to fiber is——

Senator KLOBUCHAR. And do you know that Senator Graham and I have a bill to try to do something about it?

Mr. BANKS. Well, we have worked with your staff and Senator Graham's staff. We are active with a number of State commission groups. The copper theft problem is a real problem because you don't know your copper is gone until you pick up the phone and it doesn't work.

Senator KLOBUCHAR. Mm-hmm.

Mr. BANKS. So I think you are illustrating that disasters—there is a large range of disasters, and it is hard to balance all of this.

But the movement to fiber is important, and I think it is really consumer education. The FCC has a CSRIC group devoted to studying back-up power best practices and how best to inform consumers and things. So I do think it is like we need to work together on doing the education and understanding the benefits of the transition.

Senator KLOBUCHAR. Of the copper to fiber?

Mr. BANKS. Yes.

Senator KLOBUCHAR. Mm-hmm.

Mr. BANKS. And reducing copper theft.

Senator KLOBUCHAR. Thank you. Well——

Mr. BANKS. We are in favor of that.

Senator KLOBUCHAR.—we really want to get that bill passed because, as you know, it is not just because telephone lines——

Mr. BANKS. Yes.

Senator KLOBUCHAR.—it is also about buildings and infrastructure, and they have broken into a lot of electric companies.

We have substantial support from every police group, and we are working with the veterans community because we have seen thefts from veterans' graves of medals on the graves, 200 in Isanti County in Minnesota alone. Some just this past week because of the value of copper, and yet the scrap metal dealers lobby is stopping the bill——

Mr. BANKS. Right, right.

Senator KLOBUCHAR.—on the floor and have put a hold on it, basically, through Senators. And so, anything you can do to help, we would appreciate. All it does, as you know, is require a check be written when it is over $100, the purchase, so that the police can track down, when they need to, who it is that is bringing the copper in.

Many states have those rules in place, but a number of states don't. And so, what people are doing is stealing copper from whatever source—electric companies, telephone lines, veterans' graves—and then bringing it to other states that don't have the rules in place, and it's just an outrage, and that—the bill won't go through given the widespread support we have from the business community and others.

So I am just talking about it every single day until people start to see that this is the kind of bill that is bipartisan, with Senator Hoeven and Senator Schumer and others, that needs to get done and that they should stop holding the bill up.

So, thank you. I see that Senator Booker is here, and I am going to turn it over to him.

Thank you.

STATEMENT OF HON. CORY BOOKER, U.S. SENATOR FROM NEW JERSEY

Senator BOOKER. Thank you so much, Senator.

First of all, I want to thank you all for being here. Forgive me for running in late. But I just think this is a critically important issue that we are discussing, and actually, Senator, I think your issue is an incredibly important one. I can tell you stories about copper theft from my days as a mayor.

You know, Superstorm Sandy actually came into our area, and folks in New Jersey and New York area are very, very familiar with it. And the communications networks and problems that I witnessed firsthand were particularly severe during that time, and we experienced power outages, and wireless and wireline services were unavailable due to flooding and other storm conditions, of which I know you all are very familiar.

As this technology transition moves forward, I just think it is paramount that we have reliable, consistent access to these critical safety resources like 911 and others, which, again, I am sure you all are very familiar with this.

What was made crystal clear in the experiences we saw in my region, in places like Fire Island, New York, and Mantoloking, New Jersey, is how technology transitions can pretty significantly impact consumers in ways that is not always evident at the outset, and there have been a lot of very strong feelings about this. And so, I guess the first question would be, simply, do you agree that there are many instances in which a copper network must be maintained because IP services do not meet all the needs of consumers? And that is a really open question to the panel.

Ms. GRIFFIN. Thank you.

I would say that we need to maintain the protections of the networks that we have now, as we are figuring out what the new technologies are and what opportunities we have to make sure that they are serving the same values as the existing networks did.

As you mentioned, after Hurricane Sandy in Fire Island and Mantoloking, New Jersey, Verizon decided to replace its copper network with a fixed wireless service, and there was an outcry from everybody because people really cared, and they realized that this service wasn't as good as what they had on the copper service. People had heart monitors, security systems, Internet access that they lost because the fixed wireless service didn't offer it.

And luckily, the FCC and the State commission there, in New York at least, were able to step in and protect consumers, and Verizon is now deploying fiber instead. But we still need to make sure that consumers know the differences between these technologies and are prepared for more outages.

Senator BOOKER. Somebody want to—yes, Ms. Smith?

Ms. SMITH. Yes, if I may contact—or comment as well? Public safety's view is that it is so important to maintain, and I am echoing Ms. Griffin, on exactly what they get now. They—it needs to be seamless when we move towards this transition.

But the other thing, as far as public safety is concerned, is we are excited for the future, and we look to see the improvements. Anything, the capabilities to improve communications is so important. But currently, yes, absolutely, we need to maintain what the expectations are from our consumers.

Senator BOOKER. And maintaining that means maintaining the copper, correct? Or no?

Ms. SMITH. If that—if that means maintaining——

Senator BOOKER. Can you push your button, please?

Ms. SMITH. Oh, I am sorry. Yes, if that means maintaining it at this point, yes. But again, knowing that as the future approaches, that we need to look at those capabilities and what we can do to improve.

Senator BOOKER. OK. Any other thoughts?

Ms. HONORABLE. Senator, thank you for the question, and certainly NARUC would concur.

Our core objective is safety and ensuring the safety of the people that we serve. And to respond to some of the tenets that you have mentioned in your remarks, coordination of this effort is important. We have learned so much from Hurricane Sandy.

Our National Association of Utility Commissioners, NARUC, issued a resolution after Hurricane Sandy, calling for better coordination, heightened coordination, not only with regard to mutual assistance and how the utilities have traditionally worked, what do we do in response to a storm of such a magnitude as Hurricane Sandy? What are we doing to educate the public?

And we are—we believe that the—we are technology neutral. So whatever the platform might be, the consumer comes to expect a certain level of service, a certain level of quality of service, certain consumer protections, and we support continuing that. We also support preparedness efforts, coordinating among the electric sector, the telecom sector, the Departments of Emergency Response throughout the country, county and local officials.

We also, too, want to ensure reliability. That is our core mission, as economic regulators, ensuring safe, reliable, and affordable utility service.

Senator BOOKER. And I guess my response is that we all want the same—we all have the same ambition and the same goals. My concern, especially as we get into hurricane season again, which means that the Gulf Coast and the East Coast could see another major weather event, is how do we—are we stress testing?

How are we sure that as we go through this time of transition, that we don't have more vulnerable communities that can find themselves—and again, as a guy who was in the trenches, sort of, with my first responders trying to deal with this crisis, it really is a difference between life and death.

And so, my worry is, is not that we—that we are not all affirmatively desirous of the same thing, but what are we doing to—during this time of transition to ensure that we get the result that we all want?

Ms. HONORABLE. Senator, I believe the work that we are doing is the work we do in advance, the work we do proactively. In Arkansas, as I am sure it is in New Jersey, we work proactively around tabletop exercises. I will participate in one this month, in which we are very focused on continuity of operations efforts and ramping up the broad range of potentials.

So it is a hurricane in your part of the country. For us, it is ice storms and tornados, and any other severe weather event that might occur, as well as other attacks on the grid or disruptions to the grid. But we believe that the core effort has to be proactive.

Senator BOOKER. No, and I agree. I am sorry to interrupt. And I had the privilege and pleasure of being in your state this weekend and surveyed the tornado damage in Mayflower.

I guess, to be even more specific with my question, and anybody on the panel can pick this up, is that I don't want us to be doing conversions that are creating problems that we could be anticipating and that we or that FCC, frankly, could be helping us to avoid. And so, what happened in Mantoloking and Fire Island is that we made a technology switch that proved far less reliable, especially in a crisis. Consumers not only didn't get what they want, but I felt that they were much more exposed to a crisis.

And so, I guess what I am saying is that I understand. I have gone through my—my team has gone through our tabletop exercises ad nauseam, as you should do when you are in the field and dealing from an executive position at local government. But I guess my concern is on this technology transfer—transition, how do we make sure that we are avoiding—and if we are seeing that we are creating a situation that is ripe for a crisis to emerge, how are we not deciding not to do that or not to do that transition from copper, for example?

Mr. SCHULZRINNE. Let me—thank you for the interesting question. Let me address it from two technical perspectives.

As others have alluded to, in principle, rain and fiber are a much better combination than water and copper. So, in long term, I believe, and particularly in flooding-prone areas, the goal should be that we have a fiber-dominated network simply because it will continue to function even when flooded.

The other aspect is that as communities plan their utility infrastructure, considering burial of utilities, particularly as they transition to fiber, would probably make the infrastructure much more reliable. So coordinating, and this is for long term perspective, as we do road repairs and roadwork, so that utilities, particularly fiber-based utilities, are planned for—dig-once type of policies, coordination between communication providers and the local department of public works—so that conduits are buried, for example, when roads are opened up.

That, besides opening up new opportunity for higher bandwidth communication, also, I believe, will facilitate the deployment of much more robust infrastructure that is not susceptible to wind damage and is much more resilient when water comes flooding in.

Senator BOOKER. OK. All right. And allow me to push forward, if I can, with one more question, with the permission of the chair.

One of the things I am concerned about is the penetration then of those changes, and I agree with the technology shifts. Ultimately, I think I am in concurrence with what you are saying. That is the ultimate goal. During a time of transition, I am worried about holes or gaps.

But if I can go down that way of this idea of the penetration we are seeing sort of equally applied. You know, access to technology is, to me, a great democratizing force in our society. It is powerful in terms of being a ladder for social and economic mobility.

But there are—right now, there are really significant discrepancies in the adoption and availability of a lot of these technologies, such as broadband, in lower income communities. And so, I am concerned about that these communities are often the vulnerable populations and that they are often adversely affected by technology transitions.

And so, the question very simply is, is what can we do—what should we be doing to ensure that reliable voice and broadband services are delivered to the public, regardless of economic background or geography?

Mr. BANKS. Well, if I can just jump in a little bit? I think it is really two questions. One question is the—the rural question. How can you get these facilities that are very expensive built in very rural areas? And that the FCC and a number of states have Universal Service Funds that help get infrastructure built.

The other question, the adoption question, is really a question that there has been a lot of study of, whether it is at NTIA, at FCC, states, Pew, many places. And there seems to be a real consensus that there are a couple of barriers to adoption. One is, you know, having a computer or a smartphone. Does a family have one of those?

Education is important. There are, for whatever reason, a chunk of Americans who believe the Internet does not offer value to them. And, you know, an education effort with them is important.

There are a lot of programs for adoption. The FCC is considering helping to fund or create an E-Rate program for broadband adoption. So there is a lot going on that recognizes what you are illustrating, that there is an adoption issue in America.

Senator BOOKER. And so, you are saying that the research is showing that the issue, some of it has to do with the end user's lack of appreciation or access to some of the—to laptops or to smartphones. But then—but some of your answer indicates that it is on us as well, that we are not getting it to the end user in the way that we could be?

Mr. BANKS. Certainly in rural areas it is a challenge to build networks where there are very, very few people, and that is where the availability gap would be.

Senator BOOKER. And is the shortfall—and again, I am just looking for action steps to address this, and there are a lot of conversations I am having with folks that are trying to make cheap laptops available for students, and really exciting things going on. But on the getting the technology to that end user, give me your sort of unbiased appreciation of the Universal Service Funds. Do we have the resources necessary to take on that end of the issue, and if not, what would—what is a more realistic approach?

Mr. BANKS. Well, the FCC is in the middle of reforming the USF fund to make it more efficient and more focused. So I think if they can get that operationalized and in the field, we will really be able to see if there is enough money in that fund. There is about $4.5 billion in the high-cost fund that is devoted to expanding availability.

Senator BOOKER. And can you just for a Senator that is sort of new, can you tell me what some of the issues that you are working on to make that fund more efficient?

Mr. BANKS. How best to target funding. How best to identify areas that really need the funding, versus areas that can get by without it. The current fund is sort of an old fund that allocates money in kind of unusual ways. This is a much more modern, targeted fund with a cost model to focus the money.

Senator BOOKER. Unusual ways. That sounds like a euphemism. [Laughter.]

Mr. BANKS. Well, the old fund sort of was built on a series of implicit subsidies that were not well quantified, and in the funds itself, particularly for the larger carriers, was based on statewide averaging, so that you could have a state with dense areas that, on average, would seem like it didn't need funding, although there could be parts of the state that could be very rural that did need funding.

So we are trying to target the funding much more accurately now.

Senator BOOKER. OK. I am grateful. Thank you very much.

Senator KLOBUCHAR. OK, very good.

Well, I want to thank our witnesses and thank Senator Pryor for holding this hearing, and Senator Wicker.

And we will keep the record open for 2 weeks for questions. It was a really interesting discussion with a lot more work to do.

And the hearing is adjourned. Thank you to our witnesses.

[Whereupon, at 10:42 a.m., the hearing was adjourned.]

APPENDIX

RESPONSE TO WRITTEN QUESTIONS SUBMITTED BY HON. MARK PRYOR TO HENNING SCHULZRINNE

Question 1. What measures are being taken by the FCC to protect consumers who use services such as alarms, health monitoring, and other personal emergency response services as the IP transition is taking place, as well as after the transition?

Answer. There are three separate technical issues that affect the services you describe during the transition, depending on the nature of the services and the transition. These issues are, in part, raised in a recent FCC Notice of Proposed Rulemaking (NPRM) (FCC 14–185 [1]). The three main technical concerns are:

> *Transition from landline to wireless-only:* If carriers cease to offer landline residential voice services, services that rely on either voice-data (modem) or DSL may not be able to continue to function. This issue arose when Verizon announced plans, later abandoned, to offer only 3G wireless service to residents of Fire Island, New York, after Hurricane Sandy had severely damaged the island's wireline infrastructure.

> *Analog terminal adapter incompatibility:* Devices that rely on voice modem services for low-speed data may not function properly with some analog terminal adapters (ATAs) that are used to connect in-home devices to landline VoIP networks. Such adapters are typically built into cable modems. There is currently no interoperability testing mechanisms or certifications for such devices, so that making modem-based devices work with such systems is a trial-and-error process. The FCC's Technological Advisory Council (TAC) has raised this issue recently; the Commission intends to follow up to encourage industry standards and interoperability organizations, such as ATIS, TIA or CableLabs, to take on this challenge.

Battery backup: If commercial power fails, alarm systems, even those with their own backup power, will only function if the ATA and cable or DSL modems provide backup power. The NPRM cited above asks how consumers can best be protected against such outages, *e.g.,* by allowing use of standard consumer batteries or USB power packs instead of special-purpose lead acid batteries. (Currently, some cable and DSL modems with ATA functionality include battery backup functionality. The duration of coverage varies, but is typically eight hours.)

Each of these issues requires a different approach. Some alarm systems, for example, can use cellular data services, but this may not work where cellular coverage is unavailable or the signal is too weak for indoor coverage. In roughly 85 percent of the country, consumers may be able to switch to a VoIP service offered by the local cable company if the incumbent LEC no longer offers landline voice. The table below summarizes which of the two main technology transition options may cause the issues noted above.

Transition	Low-speed data	ATA compatibility	Power backup
Landline-to-fiber	available	✓	✓
Landline-to-cellular	may not be available		✓

Question 1a. Additionally, how is the FCC working with network operators and others to promote functionality of these services on fiber optic networks just as they have on traditional copper networks?

Answer. As noted above, two separate technical problems need to be addressed, namely the ability to use low-speed data over voice channels and the power backup problem. The NPRM asks how to best solve the power backup problem. For many

---

[1] *http://www.fcc.gov/document/fcc-takes-consumer-competition-911-safeguards-tech-transitions-1*

54

networks, ATAs appear to work well with low-speed data services such as alarms, but we have no good estimate on whether problems are indeed isolated or more common. I believe that the technology transition trials will provide quantitative evidence and opportunities to assess the best approach. I encourage alarm equipment vendors to work with carriers and ATA vendors to improve interoperability through industry standards bodies.

RESPONSE TO WRITTEN QUESTIONS SUBMITTED BY HON. CORY BOOKER TO HENNING SCHULZRINNE

Question 1. Because most alarm systems currently depend on traditional telephone services, as we move to IP-networks, it is important that we consider compatibility issues and the implications for homeowners and businesses reliant on alarm systems for safety. I am concerned that consumers moving to IP networks will unknowingly disconnect their alarm systems and leave their homes and businesses vulnerable. How will IP providers work with consumers to avoid instances of unintentional system disruptions and ensure a smooth IP transition that does not compromise safety?

Answer. Please see the response to Chairman Pryor's question for general background. There are three kinds of IP (or VoIP) providers: (1) ILECs that transition from landline service to VoIP (*e.g.,* Verizon FiOS Digital Voice in New Jersey); (2) cable companies that offer voice services; and (3) over-the-top VoIP companies.

The NPRM includes proposals to update rules protecting consumers faced with network changes and discontinuance of service as the transition moves forward. Ensuring consumers have the information they need to make informed decisions is one of the top goals of the NPRM.

Question 2. Alarm systems connected via traditional telephone service have line seizure capabilities that enable the systems to communicate with monitoring stations in the event of an emergency and allow for the timely dispatch of emergency services. What are the line seizure capabilities of VoIP networks?

Answer. There are two cases: In the most common case, the residential VoIP connection simply connects to the inside analog phone wiring. In that case, assuming proper installation, the alarm system still retains the same line seizure capabilities as before.[2] Some over-the-top residential interconnected VoIP services may connect directly to a cordless or corded phone, or use a software phone. In those cases, the alarm system would have no access to the phone service at all. Many commercial (*e.g.,* small business) VoIP systems have IP-based end systems that connect to the VoIP system (PBX) via Ethernet. In that case, having a separate device that connects only to the alarm system would be advisable, as VoIP PBX can easily place multiple simultaneous calls for the same number.

RESPONSE TO WRITTEN QUESTION SUBMITTED BY HON. MARK PRYOR TO JONATHAN BANKS

Question. Some features that work for the traditional network based phone services (such as alarm signaling) may no longer work once the IP Transition is complete. How are your member companies working with consumers to ensure they are well informed about the functionality of these services over IP-based networks?

Answer. In most cases, customers will gain functionality rather than losing it when they migrate to IP-based services. A fully IP-based network provides a more efficient platform than traditional communications networks, and one that is far more flexible for innovation in services and how they are provided to customers. As a general rule, customers can continue to use fax machines, medical monitoring devices, home alarms, and accessibility services in a manner similar to what they experienced with traditional TDM service. For example, millions of customers across the country are currently using alarm systems with IP-based services.

Our industry is working to ensure a smooth transition to fully IP-based networks and services in several ways. Customers are informed of the functionality of their services during the ordering and provisioning process. Customers receive detailed information about those changes during initial contacts with a company's representatives and again at the time of installation. Technicians are trained to work through

---

[2] In standard residential landline alarm systems, the outside phone line is connected to a special jack ("RJ31X") for the alarm system, which in turn connects to the phone jacks in the home. Since the special jack is first in line, the alarm system can disconnect other phones in the home and seize the line if needed.

issues related to services that may require special handling (*e.g.,* home alarm systems) during installations. Information is also generally provided on a company's website or in a product guide. AT&T, as part of the wire center trials that it is conducting in Florida and Alabama, has begun a special community outreach effort to educate consumers about the IP Transition and any changes that may come about as older technologies are replaced with newer IP-based technologies.

In addition, our industry is working with standards bodies to address a range of potential public safety issues raised as we transition to more modern IP-based networks. For example, the Alliance for Telecommunications Industry Solutions announced in June of this year the formation of the IP-Transition of Public Safety Related Applications Task Force. The press release announcing the formation of the task force notes that "the task force will work with a broad array of industry associations to analyze the issues central to transitioning critical public safety communications infrastructure to All-IP technologies. Based on its findings, the Task Force will make targeted recommendations to both public safety and industrial associations and state and local regulators. It will also engage in outreach and education efforts to the professionals who manage critical circuits to increase their understanding of and confidence in the evolution to next generation communications.

Our industry is committed to ensuring that the transition to more modern communications networks protects public safety and supports the services that consumers want and value.

○

www.ingramcontent.com/pod-product-compliance
Lightning Source LLC
Chambersburg PA
CBHW080607180526

45168CB00007B/2816